D1267764

EATING OUT
IN·ITALY

EATING OUT IN·ITALY

BY

DIANE SEED

ILLUSTRATED BY

ROBERT BUDWIG

TEN SPEED PRESS

For Nicola, Caroline and Georgina

Edited by Maureen Green
Designed by Robert Budwig
Copy edited by Norma MacMillan
Artwork by Pep Rieff
Typesetting by Martin Delaney & Lisa Garth, TypeArt, London
Origination by Peak Litho Plates, Ltd., Tunbridge Wells
Printed in Italy by G. Canale & Co., SpA, Turin

Copyright © 1989 Diane Seed

Illustration copyright © 1989 Robert Budwig

Published in 1989 by Ten Speed Press
P.O. Box 7123, Berkeley, California 94707
First published in Great Britain in 1989 by:
Rosendale Press Limited, 140 Rosendale Road,
London SE21 8LG

All rights reserved. No part of this publication
may be reproduced, stored in a retrieval system,
or transmitted, in any form or by any means,
electronic, mechanised, photocopying,
recording, or otherwise, without the prior
permission of the copyright owner.

ISBN 0-89815-286-0
Library of Congress Number
LC 88-051936

Acknowledgements

I should like to thank Dr. Antonio Capalbi who has shared many memorable meals with me over the years. While I was working on this book he endured a very unbalanced diet consisting of demanding gourmet weekends followed by haphazard meals at home with comparative equanimity.

It would be invidious to single out any owner or chef featured in this book as they have all been particularly enthusiastic and helpful in discussing their work and in offering recipes, and my thanks go to them all.

Over the years many friends and acquaintances have shared their gastronomic expertise with me, but I would like to thank the following for their help: in Puglia, Licia, Elia and Mario Longo, Anna and Elio Della Notte, Sandra and Lucio Della Notte; in Naples, Pupa and Lucio Sicca and Pamela Holding; in Ischia, Lady Walton; in Turin, Giacomo Canale, in Venice, Sally Spector and the late Giuseppe Maffioli whose book, "La Cucina Veneziana" is so informative; in Rome, Jack Buckley and Audris D'Aragona.

My editor, Maureen Green, has been unfailingly helpful and supportive and my British publisher, Timothy Green, has kept me company on some of the eating out. Pamela Burden has calmly and efficiently typed and retyped the manuscript and Jonquil and Edward Barr have been punctilious proof-readers.

As always, my special thanks to Robert Budwig who has put so much of himself into the "Eating Out in Italy" experience.

Diane Seed, Rome, 1989

CARTA D'ITALIA

TORINO
MILANO
VENEZIA
GENOVA
BOLOGNA
FIRENZE
ROMA
NAPOLI
LECCE

Contents

Introduction

*I*talian food is the product of one of the world's greatest cooking traditions. The warmth of Italian life, which thrives on eating out regularly with family and friends to enjoy good food in a pleasurable setting, has created an unequalled choice of restaurants throughout the country. In every region, formal and elegant gastronomic shrines are to be found surrounded and outnumbered by cheerful trattorias overlooking seas, lakes and historic buildings.

Due to its long history as a series of separate kingdoms, and city states, Italy today, although unified politically since 1861, still produces food which is firmly rooted in its regional traditions. Italian food as such scarcely exists, but the cooking of Tuscany or Naples or Piedmont has a flavour of its own. The pleasure for the traveller is to know that the menu changes not just from restaurant to restaurant, but is transformed from region to region. For this reason, each chapter is introduced with a general explanation of the food of that region.

So great is the choice in Italy, that the visitor needs a guide less to avoid eating badly, than to be able to seek out the most exciting and unusual experiences that Italy has to offer. In this guide, I have brought together my favourite restaurants, trattorias, bars and cafes, discovered as a result of twenty years of living in Rome and exploring throughout Italy the best that can be found. The visitor who picks a restaurant from this book, in whatever price range, should find pleasure and value for money. *Buon appetito!*

The Italian Menu

In many relaxed, comparatively inexpensive restaurants, there is no written menu. The waiter or owner tells you the day's special dishes. Even when a written menu exists, Italian customers rely more on verbal suggestions. More expensive restaurants give a menu so that you are aware of the higher prices, and often such restaurants tend to give women a menu without prices – a habit I deplore. The Italian menu, presented in restaurants and trattorias, is worth many minutes of study. However, it is set out in a way that may not always be clear to visitors.

Antipasti, which may range from such standbys as parma ham and melon, (now adapted by restaurants all over the world) through every kind of individual concoction of the chef, are designed to take the edge off the appetite and accompany the first glass of wine. In some restaurants, however, especially in the Piedmont region, up to a dozen antipasti may be offered and the visitor will have to exercise restraint to get any further.

In fact, these little dishes are not really considered a formal part of the meal, for *I Primi*, or the First Course, may be a choice of pasta or rice or soup, even a light vegetable dish, according to the region. The main course, of meat or fish, is therefore *I Secondi*, or the Second Course. Chicken, veal, beef, lamb, game as well as many kinds of local fish will all appear at this point, as well as many vegetable dishes and salads that are among the best in the world.

The last course in most Italian restaurants is the sweet course, *I Dolci*, although in Piedmont, in the north, the excellent local cheeses are on offer, and in Puglia (in the 'heel') tender celery and fennel are presented as an alternative to fruit as a final course. As well as the many Italian desserts based on chestnuts, ricotta, almonds and sponge cake, Italian fruit, in its abundance and range, offers strong competition, and many visitors may well prefer to end the meal with *frutta fresca* (fresh fruit) in every region.

Wine: The range and quality of Italian wines has established a new reputation over the last ten years. In each area, some of the best vineyards and types of wine have been indicated in the regional introductions.

Coffee: Italian coffee, black (*caffè* or *espresso*), is always served at the end of the meal. For less concentrated coffee, order a *caffè lungo*, or *caffè macchiato*, 'stained' with a few drops of cold milk. Coffee with milk (*capuccino*) is basically a morning drink.

Prices: In this guide, restaurant prices are indicated as 'expensive', 'moderate', or 'inexpensive', with some shaded in between, such as 'moderate to expensive'. By 'inexpensive' , we mean a total price of Lire 25,000 or less, per person, without wine. 'Moderate' indicates a total price, per person, without wine, of Lire 25,000 to 50,000. 'Expensive' means over Lire 50,000 per person without wine. Nowadays it is quite possible to pay over Lire 100,000 per person, without wine, in the most exclusive restaurants. These higher prices throughout Italy have come about partly because restaurants are now required by law to issue every customer with a formal bill. *Please note:* by law the customer must leave the restaurant with a bill. The legal onus is on the customer to produce the bill if asked to do so by the authorities. Failure to do so can result in a fine.

Service: A service charge is always built into the total price of the menu, whether this is mentioned or not. However, a very little more, a *mancia*, is normally left on the table (somewhere between Lire 3,000 to 10,000 not more) by happy customers.

VITERBO

ANGUILLARA

ROMA

TIVOLI

FIUMINCINO

LIDO DI OSTIA

ROME
& the surrounding towns

*I*n Rome the great universal pleasure is eating out. Every
other form of entertainment takes second place. If you see an
animated group of men enjoying a lively discussion on
Monday morning they are inevitably talking about
Sunday's football and what they ate over the weekend.
Rome has more eating places than any other Italian city and
centuries of democracy have made '*la gola*' (the palate) the
great leveller. All walks of life meet at adjoining tables and
the waiters treat every customer as an equal with complete
informality. There is a general feeling of gaiety and pleasure
in which everyone participates. Whole families eat out
together and every trattoria has several high chairs for small
children. Babies are passed round the table which often
seats four generations of the same family. Among friends,

dinner parties at home are quite rare; instead, groups of four or five couples arrange to eat out together. Most of the dining-rooms are well-lit and simple, with pride of place given to great still-life groupings of food.

In the last few years there has been a certain amount of change. Several more sophisticated restaurants with soft lights and elegant decor have become fashionable and some of these serve excellent food, like *Il'Tentativo* in Trastevere, Via della Luce 5 (tel. 589 5234), closed lunch and Sundays. However, there have been a few less successful metamorphoses and whereas it was once quite difficult to eat badly in Rome, nowadays you have to be a little more wary about prices and choose more carefully.

Rome enjoys a delightful climate and from early spring to late autumn lunchtime sees tables arranged outside on pavements, courtyards and cobbled piazzas. In the really warm months one of the great pleasures is dining in an historic square surrounded by mellow, tawny buildings, still lit by old-fashioned street lamps. One restaurant with such a classic setting is *Pino e Dino*, piazza di Montevecchio, off via Coronari (tel. 686 1319), closed Mondays.

On Sundays and public holidays Romans traditionally eat '*fuori porta*', or outside the old city walls. They usually head for the sea at Ostia or Fiumicino or drive out to the small wine-producing towns grouped round the extinct volcanoes which form Lake Nemi and Lake Albano, an area known as the 'Castelli Romani'. The volcanic soil here is very fertile, and since ancient times this area has been famous for its food and wine. Much of Cicero's rhetoric was fuelled by the local wine when he lived in Frascati and the Pope traditionally retires to Castel Gandolfo in the summer months to gain new strength and inspiration. At the height of summer the area is comparatively cool and refreshing and in cold weather there are blazing wood fires in the dining-rooms of the local trattorias. Nemi, once sacred to the goddess Diana, is famous for its small sweet strawberries. Ariccia produced the first *porchetta* which is now found everywhere; a six month old pig flavoured with sage and rosemary and spit-roasted whole. Those wanting to feast on *funghi porcini* come to the area around Velletri; the huge restaurant *Da Baffone*, Via dei Laghi (15 kilometres from central Rome) is so famous for this delicacy that the owner is nicknamed 'the king of the ceps'. (Tel. 963 3892)

Traditional Roman cooking is tasty yet simple with no subtle or imaginative twists. It is essentially the robust, masculine cooking you would expect from ancient Republican Rome and there is no hint of the decadence of Imperial Rome or later Papal excesses. The courtly influence seems non-existent and what we find today is the cooking of the people, plain and direct with strong, pungent flavours. The Roman soldier's love of garlic was legendary; '*Ubi Roma ibi allium*' (wherever Romans go, there is garlic), and today garlic is the main ingredient in snacks like *bruschetta* – coarse bread toasted, sprinkled with olive oil then rubbed vigorously with garlic – and the ubiquitous quick pasta dish *spaghetti aglio, olio e peperoncino* (garlic, olive oil, chilli).

Vegetables play an important part in Roman cooking and many green, leafy vegetables are cooked simply in water then either served cold, *all'agro* with lemon juice and olive oil or heated *in padella*, with garlic and chilli pepper. Rome has a pointed green cauliflower known as *broccolo romano*, bitter greens, *cicoria*, and the more usual spinach and chard – *bieta*. An interesting vegetable *puntarella*, is served as a salad with a sauce made of pounded garlic and anchovies. A mixed green salad can contain as many as six different green leaves. The ornamental *pinzimonio* consists of celery, fennel, carrots, radishes and cucumber accompanied by a bowl of oil and vinegar dressing. The vegetables are dipped into the communal bowl of dressing and nibbled, then dipped again, much to the consternation of the health-conscious. Young broad beans or *fave* are usually eaten raw with pecorino romano cheese and traditionally served on May 1st. The *carciofi alla romana* (globe artichoke) look spectacular served standing on their heads with the long stalks in the air. The artichokes are stuffed with mint and braised in oil and white wine. Another very good artichoke dish comes from the old Roman ghetto, *carciofi alla giudia*, for which the artichoke is flattened then deep fried. Because very young artichokes are used it is possible to eat every morsel. Other Jewish specialities which have been absorbed into Roman cooking are fried fillets of *baccalà* (salt cod) and *fiori di zucca*, marrow (squash) flowers stuffed with mozzarella cheese and a little anchovy before being deep-fried.

Romans love their homemade egg pasta, *fettuccine*, but they are also happy with *pasta asciutta* (flour and water paste), and their two favourite dishes are *spaghetti alla carbonara* and *spaghetti alla matriciana*. Both these sauces use bacon, *guanciale*, cut from the pig's cheek or jowl.

Roman pizza is extremely good and light because the dough is rolled out very thinly to form a very crisp crust. Individual pizzas are only served in the evening, but during the day small speciality shops prepare *pizza rustica*, large flat trays of pizza with various toppings which provide a delicious, inexpensive snack. Another inexpensive snack is *supplì*, rice balls filled with mozzarella cheese, rolled in breadcrumbs and deep fried. When you bite into them the melted mozzarella stretches into strings like telephone lines, hence the name. One inexpensive haunt, *La Fiorentina*, Via Andrea Doria, 18 (tel. 359 8195) closed Wednesday, serves all these specialities.

The great Roman meat dish is *abbacchio* or very young milk-fed lamb. This was true even in ancient Rome when Juvenal describes a dinner party where he served a lamb 'more full of milk than blood'. The *abbacchio* is either roasted or the tiny chops are grilled and then eaten with the hands *'scottadito'* – to burn the fingers. Young kid, *capretto*, is also a firm favourite. Beef and veal used not to be eaten in the past but now they are generally present

on every menu especially *saltimbocca alla romana*, made of thin slices of veal topped with ham and a sprig of sage, rolled up and then fried. Traditionally, Roman cooking makes superlative use of the cheaper cuts of meat. Tripe, *trippa* and *pajata*, parts of the intestines, makes savoury dishes and oxtail is used for the legendary *coda alla vaccinara*.

Wine served in the carafe usually comes from the Castelli region and white is most common. Although restaurant wine lists are improving, this area of Italy does not produce great wines. Most trattorias, however, still offer a free *digestivo* at the end of the meal, most commonly *amaro*, a bitter herbal liqueur, or *sambuca*, a clear aniseed-flavoured drink. This is served traditionally with coffee beans (always

an odd number for luck) which are known as *la mosca* or the fly. These are meant to be crunched as you drink the liqueur to make an interesting combination of tastes.

Rome is full of little bars, where the population can be seen leaning against the counter to down a morning *caffè* with a pastry, or sampling a liqueur at night. One of the more distinguished cafés with a long history (Casanova, Shelley and Goethe were all here) is the *Caffè Greco*, at Via Condotti 86, not far from the Spanish Steps. The *Caffè* is lively all week, but closed on Sundays.

In Rome you can lunch from 1 pm, but many customers arrive as late as 2.30 pm. In the evening, pizzerias open at 7 pm but most restaurants start serving dinner from 8 to 8.30 pm and continue until very late into the night.

In Rome, as in many large cities, it is advisable to leave valuables behind and handbags are at risk in many areas. Trastevere and 'old' Rome, with their narrow streets, are particularly vulnerable to thieves on motor scooters.

Mario
Via della Vite 56, Rome
Tel. 673 3818

Via della Vite is in the very centre of Rome's shopping area, two minutes from the Piazza di Spagna and Via Frattina. At Number 56, next to the Anglo-American Bookshop, we find an honest, reasonably-priced trattoria, owned by Tuscan-born Mario Mariani. Mario started his professional life working in hotels but in 1960 he realised a long-standing ambition and took over a small, failing pizzeria, turning it into the thriving trattoria it is today. His parents moved from Tuscany to help him in the restaurant's early years and his 90 year-old mother lives with him and his family above the restaurant, still giving an occasional word of advice and a hand with the traditional desserts. This helps give the trattoria its family feeling, as indeed do the waiters, some of whom have been with Mario for over 20 years. Despite the move to Rome, the family retains house, land and strong roots in Tuscany and the trattoria serves traditional Tuscan food and wine. Large bottles of chianti classico stand on all the tables and the customer pays only for what he drinks, the amount being calculated with a quick glance by the experienced waiters. Mario also has 10,000 numbered bottles of a fine chianti, 'La Canonica', produced for him every year and usually my personal choice.

As a starter I always allow myself to be tempted by *finocchiona* – a delicious *salame* flavoured with fennel seeds. Mario also makes very appetising *crostini* (toasts). At *Mario*'s I usually ignore the pasta, although it is very good, and settle for one of the robust Tuscan soups, either *ribollita*, a thick vegetable soup or *pasta e fagioli*, pasta and beans in a dense broth. Both of these dishes usually have a little olive oil poured on top, a first pressing obtained from Mario's own olives in the Val d'Arno region.

Tuscan beans are traditionally cooked in a large glass chianti bottle called a *fiasco*. This tradition is believed to have been started by a glass-blower in Empoli. The Tuscans are highly inventive – after all, Leonardo came from Vinci in Tuscany – and this glass-blower decided to embellish his packed lunch by putting a few dried beans and a little water into a bottle he had just made and placing the sealed bottle into the glass furnace. The lunchtime beans were exquisite, word spread and the method was adopted into Tuscan culinary lore. In season *Mario* serves game, and both hare and succulent wild boar are to be found on the menu, as well as the more familiar Florentine beef steaks. I usually indulge in one of the rich casseroles, such as *stracotto* or *brasato* in which large pieces of beef have been braised in good red wine. *Capretto* or young goat is also very good, with a flavour very much like lamb but a much lower fat content.

The traditional Tuscan cakes are made fresh twice a day by Mario's wife, and the cakes are brought to the table and left for the customer to help himself to as much as he wants. One of the most famous is *castagnaccio*, made from chestnut flour with pine nuts and rosemary sprinkled on top.

Mario's is a friendly, unpretentious trattoria which has a large following of regular customers. There are 150 settings and the tables are cheerfully close together. The rooms are decorated with the odd antler or two, and strings of garlic and chillis hang over the bar. Genial Mario is always there, greeting old friends and making new customers feel welcome and at home. I like to come here for a restoring break in the middle of a shopping spree, or for a calm evening meal after a long day.

Price: *moderate to inexpensive; all major credit cards*
Closed: *Sunday; part of August*
Location: *central Rome, Piazza di Spagna*

Checccino dal 1887

Via di Monte Testaccio 30, Rome
Tel. 574 6318

Mount Testaccio is not one of the seven hills of Rome, but a hill made up of about 86 million broken Roman amphoras or jugs – hence its name, from the Latin *testa*, or terracotta. In Imperial Rome wine, oil and wheat were transported to the city by boat in large, unglazed earthenware pots which were stored in warehouses by the side of the Tiber. These amphoras were too porous to be used twice and to avoid the river being blocked by discarded pottery, the Emperor Nero issued a decree in 55 AD ordering the amphoras to be broken and stacked systematically with the neck and handles in one pile and the main piece in another. Gradually these piles built up to form a grass-covered hill reaching a height of 70 metres. Over the centuries caves were cut out of the hill for storage, since the terracotta keeps the temperature a constant 10°C and minimises humidity.

The trattoria, *Checcino dal 1887*, which has just celebrated its centenary, started life as a wine shop using one of these storage caves in Mount Testaccio. In 1887 the wine shop proprietors – great-, great-grand-parents of the present owners – obtained a licence to serve simple food with their wine, and when the new slaughter-house was opened nearby in 1890 their success was assured. Part of the slaughter-house workers' pay consisted of the

quinto quarto, fifth quarter – the intestines, tail, feet, etc. which had no commercial value. The workers took these humble parts to the trattoria to be cooked and somehow made edible. Ferminia, the daughter, was an ingenious cook and she invented many tasty dishes, including the famous *coda alla vaccinara* made with oxtail. Over the years many other trattoria sprang up, all using these cheap cuts and serving what was known as *cucina povera* or poor food, which has come to be regarded as one of the glories of Roman cooking.

Today, *Checchino*, run by the same family, still serves traditional Roman food. The decor remains simple and unpretentious but the exquisite wine glasses reflect the new elegance, and the present clientele includes well-known figures from the world of politics and the arts. Some of the old recipes have been made lighter to suit modern palates, and more expensive cuts of meat have been added to the menu – excellent steaks and grills – to please customers who have not developed a taste for the *quinto quarto*.

I confess I usually avoid the renowned *pajata* – small intestines and settle for spaghetti with one of the delicious, very Roman sauces, such as *amatriciana*, made from tomatoes, bacon and pecorino cheese. All the vegetables served in the restaurant are grown without artificial fertilizers and the veal stuffed with artichokes has a wonderful flavour. Their speciality, *coda alla vaccinara*, is still made from Ferminia's original recipe. Ninette Mariani who reigns in the kitchen makes excellent icecream, and her son Elio has built up a superb list of Italian, French and Californian wines which are still stored in the Monte Testaccio cave. His brother Francesco speaks fluent English and is always ready to help visitors choose a memorable meal.

Squeamish readers will be pleased to hear that the slaughter-house was closed in 1977, and no untoward squeals now disturb the peace of this fascinating, unusual district. It is one of my favourite Roman haunts and I love to shop in the colourful market open every morning in a neighbouring piazza. The whole area is full of little speciality shops which bustle with warmth, humour and enjoyment of life. Not far away is Cestius' pyramid, built in 12 BC and the peaceful Protestant cemetery where Keats is buried and Shelley has his memorial.

Price: *moderate to expensive; Amex*
Closed: *Sunday, Monday; August, Christmas*
Location: *near the Pyramide*

Costanza
Piazza del Paradiso 65, Rome
Tel. 686 1717

This trattoria is between S. Andrea della Valle – the church where Puccini's 'Tosca' is set and Campo dei Fiori – one of the most fascinating parts of Rome. Every morning Campo dei Fiori is the scene of a bustling food market and many of the local restaurateurs do their shopping here. The whole area has long been the centre of good eating. In one corner of Campo dei Fiori is Piazza di Biscione, the site of the colossal 17,000-seat theatre that Pompey built to celebrate his triumph in 61 BC. It was in this theatre, alongside the statue of Pompey, that Julius Caesar was murdered on the Ides of March in 44 BC. The semi-circular Via Grotta Pinta, which leads off the piazza through a dark, sinister passage between two gates, follows the line of the original amphitheatre and many of the local trattorias have rooms among the ruins of this huge theatre. *Costanza*, in Piazza del Paradiso, is one of the most gastronomically interesting.

During the summer months, tables are set outside in an intriguing picturesque little alley, but before or after dinner it is worth making a point of going inside to see the theatre ruins – ancient columns, masks and amphoras.

Costanza was taken over by Giuseppe Giovannenza, an ex-Carabinieri, and Paride di Giovanni, an ex-friar, in 1979. The two met doing military service, deciding they preferred to pursue culinary excellence rather than spiritual or temporal sinners.

I like to start with the marrow (squash) flower risotto, *risotto con fiori di zucca*, or the ravioli stuffed with chopped artichokes, *ravioli con carciofi*. Tiny lamb chops are served piping hot straight from the grill and since they are best eaten with the fingers this way is known as '*scottadito*' – literally 'to burn the fingers'. *Costanza* serves both lamb, *abbacchio* and young goat, *capretto*. In season they serve *funghi porcini*, and another house speciality is crêpes stuffed with mushrooms and truffle, or *tartufo*. Here is a good place to sample *scamorza alla griglia*, the small pear-shaped cheeses from Molise that are grilled on a spit over the fire. All the desserts are home-made and Paride and Giuseppe are always experimenting and inventing new delights for their customers.

Prices: *moderate to inexpensive; Amex, Visa*
Closed: *Sunday; part of August*
Location: *central Rome, near the Campo dei Fiori*

Vecchia Roma
Piazza Campitelli, Rome
Tel. 686 4604

My favourite time to visit *Vecchia Roma* is on a summer evening when it is possible to sit outside under the huge market umbrellas in the delightful piazza Campitelli with its Baroque fountain and church and its warm, mellow buildings. For anyone with only one such evening to spend in Rome my recipe would include *Vecchia Roma* as the main ingredient. Before dinner I suggest a gentle stroll to Piazza Mattei to admire Taddeo Landini's *Fontana delle Tartarughe* – a charming little fountain dating from the late sixteenth century. After dinner, cross over to the Campidoglio and climb the steps to admire the view of the Forum and Colosseum which have more power to thrill the imagination when seen at night without the distraction of seething hordes and endless traffic. Wander down the Via S. Pietro in Carcere reflecting on past glories. As you walk over the original sections of the old

Roman road you may be surprised to hear echoes of rhythmic marching footsteps. Legend has it that on certain nights when the wind is in the right direction the Emperor's Praetorian Guard can still be heard returning in triumph to the Capitoline Hill.

The *Vecchia Roma* restaurant is owned by the brothers Giuseppe and Toninio Palladino who, having spent several years working in London restaurants, returned to Rome in 1972 to realise their ambition and buy the long-established *Vecchia Roma*. The menu changes according to the season and they are always experimenting to invent new delicacies. My favourite pasta dishes are pennette with *zucchine*, tagliolini with lemon sauce or *bavette* (long thin noodles) with *rughetta*, the sharp salad herb known as rocket or arugula. The *funghi porcini* (large cep mushrooms), are always excellent here and you may find them fresh in a salad, served roasted as a main course or made into a heavenly sauce for pasta. Giuseppe has a secret mushroom

supplier, and an ingenious way of preserving them for sauces.

The grilled meat is consistently good, but I usually can't resist lamb with artichokes or grilled scampi. *Vecchia Roma* has recently introduced a special salad menu consisting of some twelve or more exuberant salads which have been proved very popular in a city more used to traditional vegetables. All the usual sweets are to be found on the menu, but I think top honours go to the home-made fruit sorbets.

Inside *Vecchia Roma* there are several rooms adorned with murals of old Rome. If you plan to eat inside you should specify the exact table when making your reservation. For an intimate foursome there is a table set deep into an alcove and for a romantic evening *à deux* a table near a small graceful fountain is set far from other diners. There is even a strongbox of a private room seating ten. With its own entrance and with doors and windows reinforced and soundproofed, it is ideal for heads of state or other famous or infamous characters wanting discretion.

Price: *moderate to expensive; Amex*
Closed: *Wednesday; part of August*
Location: *central Rome, near the Campidoglio*

Al Pompiere
Via S. Maria dei Calderari 38, Rome
Tel. 686 8377

In the days of Emperor Augustus the Jews in Rome enjoyed comparative tolerance. It was not until the seventeenth century and the Counter-Reformation that oppression really arrived. Pope Paul IV ordered the Roman Jews – some 3,000 – to be confined in a small area and subject to a rigid curfew. This area, near the Tiber Island, became known as the 'ghetto', probably from the Hebrew word, 'ghet' meaning separation. The ghetto was enclosed by high stone walls and originally there were only two closely guarded doorways. Some 300 years later, the walls were destroyed and the ghetto was opened up, and is now one of the most fascinating areas of Rome.

My favourite ghetto restaurant, *Pompiere*, is in the Piazza delle Cinque Scole, on the first floor of the old Cenci Palace. All Rome's Jewish specialities are to be found. It is usual to start the meal with a plate of fried salted cod (*baccalà*), marrow (squash) flowers fried in batter (*fiore di zucca ripieno*) and young artichokes which are flattened out until they resemble water lilies and then deep fried. After this those with a strong constitution can go on to one of the delightful pasta dishes such as pennette with lemon sauce, fettuccine with asparagus or spaghetti with artichoke sauce. The rest of the menu is very extensive and there are mouth-watering sweets.

Dino Monteferri who was born into the restaurant is a genial host and a great advertisement for the cooking. As he himself points out he has been eating *Pompiere* food for the last 62 years.

Price : moderate to inexpensive; credit cards not accepted
Closed: Sunday; part of August
Location: central Rome, behind the synagogue

Osteria da Nerone
Via delle Terme di Tito 96, Rome
Tel. 474 5207

Da Nerone is ideally placed near S. Pietro in Vincoli on a hill just above the Colosseum. In summer the tables are set outside on the pavement and, although the traffic winds up and down, it is easy to feel peacefully detached from the confusion after the warm welcome provided by the De Santis brothers, who come from the gastronomically famous Abruzzo. If you decide to sit outside do go into the restaurant before ordering, since the written menu gives little idea of the treats in store.

Inside, a long table is covered with a great variety of antipasti, and you take a plate and help yourself. For the pasta course, the homemade ravioli stuffed with ricotta cheese and spinach are particularly good here, served with melted-butter and sage leaves. The house speciality is *fettuccine al Nerone*, with peas, mushrooms, egg and salame. If you happen to be visiting *Da Nerone* on a Thursday (Thursday in Rome is traditionally the day for gnocchi) their light tasty gnocchi should be tried.

The Abruzzese lamb served here is renowned, and they also prepare all the usual meat dishes like *saltimbocca alla Romana*. Fresh fish is available on Tuesdays and Fridays, traditional fish days in Rome. *Da Nerone* offers very good value for money, and the atmosphere is relaxed and friendly.

Price: moderate to inexpensive; credit cards not accepted
Closed: Sunday; part of August
Location: central Rome, near the Colosseum

Sabatini

Vicolo Santa Maria in Trastevere 18, Rome
Tel. 581 8307

Trastevere is one of the most colourful areas of Rome with its narrow, cobbled streets and mellow old buildings. The heart of Trastevere is Piazza Santa Maria with its central fountain and lovely church, believed to be the oldest in Rome. The zone teems with eating places and there are two *Sabatinis*, one in the main piazza and one in the small alley just round the corner. I always go to the latter. It is dear to my heart since I ate my first Roman meal here over 20 years ago. I remember waiting for a table with other hungry would-be diners, and one of the Sabatini brothers offered us shavings of *prosciutto crudo* from his carving knife to stay our hunger pangs. Today there is the same jolly friendly atmosphere, although it is an area over-exposed to tourists, and in the evening strolling musicians provide traditional Roman songs.

In front of the entrance door there is a huge open fire where steaks, chops, fish and scampi are grilled to order. A good choice of pasta dishes is always available and all the Roman specialities can be found here, as well as good fish and other regional favourites like *osso buco*.

The house wine from the Castelli is served in colourful pottery jugs and there is a fair wine list.

Price : *Moderate to expensive; all major credit cards*
Closed: *Tuesday; part of August*
Location: *Trastevere, south of the river Tiber*

Pommidoro
Piazza dei Sanniti, Rome
Tel. 445 2692

Near the church of San Lorenzo Fuori Le Mure is the densely-populated, working-class area of S. Lorenzo. The buildings tend to be in need of a coat of paint and there are not many trees or flowering balconies to be seen but the area pulses with life.

Pommidoro is owned by Anna and Aldo Bravi and it is in every sense a family trattoria. Daughters and their husbands wait at table and the small grand-children play and squabble happily among the tables. Aldo's grandmother, Clementinona, started the family off with a simple wine shop. She was a gigantic lady – a special chair was made to accommodate her ample proportions – and she personally threw out drunken customers, two at a time. In 1926 Aldo's father started to serve food with the wine and he quickly attracted a mixed clientele of craftsmen, intellectuals and celebrities. Because he got on so well with all these different individuals, the trattoria became known in Roman dialect as *Pommidoro* since everyone in Italy knows that the tomato goes well with all other ingredients. Aldo, who started working in the trattoria when he was seven years old, has his father's gregarious nature and he also draws his customers from the nearby university and the wider worlds of art and show-business.

Midday is the best time to go to *Pommidoro* and it is possible to eat as late as 3.00 pm when most other trattoria have stopped serving lunch. Anna Bravi is an inventive cook and no dish ever tastes the same twice. She is a wizard with *funghi porcini* and some of the most memorable pasta I have ever eaten is her spaghetti with this wild mushroom. The meat is always excellent. In season they serve game shot by the Bravis themselves, and the vegetables and olive oil are produced on their land in the Sabine Hills. I usually drink their own white wine which is very pleasant.

Pommidoro does not try to be quaint or picturesque. In summer the tables are carried outside and set on the sloping pavement in a scruffy piazza surrounded by parked cars. In winter the tables are crowded inside the one eating room. I go here often, not for the atmosphere but for the good food, the friendly Bravi family and above all for the very Roman faces of the other customers. In some strange way, lunch at *Pommidoro* is like a visit to Caesar's Forum.

Price: *moderate to inexpensive; credit cards not accepted*
Closed: *Sunday; August*
Location: *San Lorenzo district*

Grotte di Livia

Piazza Saxa Rubra 9, Rome
Tel. 691 1253

On a hot evening, when central Rome proves stifling, it is tempting to escape to Prima Porta on the outskirts of Rome, where Livia Drusilla and Caesar Augustus centuries ago used to flee the heat in their villa high on a hill looking over the river Tiber. The villa was excavated in 1863 bringing to light the famous statue of Augustus now in the Vatican Museum. An underground room was discovered, almost undamaged, decorated with charming murals of a refreshing garden scene, complete with flowerbeds, green lawns and songbirds. A series of storage caves had been dug out for the villa at the foot of the hill and these provided the site for Cesare Francellini's delightful restaurant *Grotte di Livia*, which specialises in good grilled meat. The restaurant is warm and intimate in the winter and cool and refreshing in the sumner. (This restaurant is only open in the evening so it cannot be combined with a daytime outing.) In winter the tables are tucked away in intimate corners of the low tunnelled-out rooms. At the far end there is a huge fire used to grill meat and produce an endless supply of *bruschetta*. In summer the tables are more numerous, arranged in a cool courtyard around a fountain. There is a great barbecue outside set at a comfortable distance from the diners. The good wine list was chosen originally by Trimani, the renowned Roman wine merchant. In summer I usually drink a refreshingly chilled Galestro Viola, while in winter a Nebbiola or Santa Cristina Chianti will send a warm glow through the blood stream.

Home-made pasta stuffed with spinach and ricotta is always very good, and in winter I usually choose this or the pasta *alla Norcina* – with cream and sausage. In summer there is the traditional cool pasta *alla checca* made with very ripe uncooked tomatoes. The meat is always superb in this restaurant. Great succulent steaks *alla fiorentina* fill the plate and there are fillet steaks and tender veal chops for less robust appetites. Cesare's mother, Nombilia – a rare, old Etruscan name – keeps a vigilant eye on the pasta and *dolci*, and Cesare himself seems to be everywhere, often it would seem producing tables out of thin air.

Price: *moderate to expensive; credit cards not accepted*
Closed: *Monday*
Location: *16 km from central Rome, off the Via Flaminia*

Cecilia Metella
Via Appia Antica 125, Rome
Tel. 513 6743

Cecilia Metella in the Appia Antica, is idyllic on long, lazy summer evenings or as a cool lunch-time retreat when the heat of the day seems too fierce for comfort. Further up the Appia Antica where the marks from ancient Roman chariot wheels can be seen engraved in the paving stones, is the crenellated top of the tomb of Cecilia Metella – a wealthy Roman matron.

The *Cecilia Metella* trattoria has been going strong for 200 years, but the present owners, Roberto and Marcantonio Graziani from the Abruzzo – a region famous for its excellent cuisine – took over in 1965. The restaurant is at its best in the warmer months when the tables are set outside in a delightful garden complete with roses, fish pond and fountain.

The trattoria boasts two excellent inventions, among pasta dishes. *Scrigno* (literally jewel box) is made of thin tagliatelle, cheese, ham and tomatoes cooked in the oven in small, individual pottery bowls, indented at the top like miniature Cecilia Metella towers. *Zite al prosciutto* is a dish of fairly long tubes of pasta and ham in a buttery sauce. This is one of my favourites although very difficult to eat. The zite are too short to wind easily round the fork and too long to slip daintily into the mouth. Resign yourself to a buttery chin and enjoy them!

For the main course there is good plain meat and fish cooked on a large charcoal grill or more elaborate veal and chicken dishes. The sweets trolley is very tempting, with *Monte Bianco* (chestnut purée, meringue and whipped cream) a perennial favourite. There is a good wine list and the house wine, a Frascati Fontana Candida, is very pleasant.

Price: *moderate to inexpensive; Amex*
Closed: *Monday*
Location: *on Via Appia Antica*

Lido Di Ostia

*A*ny visitor to Rome who wants to see ruins to rival those of Pompeii and Herculaneum should make for Ostia Antica, Rome's ancient port now inland, (but check opening times).

Da Negri
Via Claudia 50, Lido Di Ostia
Tel. 562 2295

On the sea front at Ostia itself, there is an endless stretch of beach establishments with battalions of umbrellas and deck-chairs marching to the sea, crowded with restaurants that should be strenuously avoided, particularly in the summer. However, just a few yards from the sea front, facing Piazza della Rovere we find trattoria *Da Negri*. The restaurant was first opened 60 years ago by a sea-plane pilot and in those days there was nothing between the trattoria and the sea. Urban development has extinguished the sea view but not the tradition of good seafood.

Romano Felice, who runs this busy restaurant (open all the year) has been involved in many ventures, including the first Spoleto festival. He was part of the Roman nightclub scene for many years, but in 1982 he decided to concentrate on his Ostia restaurant. He is omnipresent, and has absorbed all his family in this enterprise. He has employed an ex-fisherman to buy first class fish from the daily fish auction at Fiumicino.

In extravagant mood one can start with oysters or a selection of delicious fish antipasti, like mussels stuffed with garlic and parsley, fried squid or mixed seafood salad. In summer I always include the delicious marrow (squash) flowers fried in batter. There follow two or three small portions of pasta or risotto usually made with *frutti di mare*. My favourites include *scampi risotto*, taglioni with smoked salmon, and a delicious version of the ubiquitous spaghetti with clams (*vongole*).

For the main course it is hard to beat the superb baked fish, and I suggest a good size *sarago* (brill) or *spigola* (sea bass) to be shared between two. The scampi and the mixed grill of fish is also very good.

Price: moderate; Amex, Diners
Closed: Thursday, except high season
Location: 24 km from Rome

Fiumicino

Fiumicino, a small fishing port, is known mainly for the international airport of Leonardo da Vinci. But nearby is one of my favourite eating places, which can make a memorable first or last meal in Rome.

Miranda
Lungomare della Salute 39, Fiumicino
Tel. 644 0077

Domenico Zafrani, Alberto's brother, has left 'Il Pescatore' to take over and upgrade a large resturant called *Miranda*, on Fiumicino's rather drab sea front. The cook also comes from 'Il Pescatore', so one finds old favourites on the menu, including the incredible *spaghetti all'aragosta*, with so many large pieces of lobster that it is almost a meal in itself. Domenico has organised everything with the professional care and attention to detail which characterises the Zafrani brothers, and the restaurant is comfortable and inviting with its profusion of graceful green plants.

Price: moderate; Amex, Visa
Closed: Monday
Location: seafront, Fiumicino, 28 km from Rome

Il Pescatore
Via Torre Clementina 154, Fiumicino
Tel. 644 0189

Il Pescatore – the fisherman – is opposite the jetty where the daily catch is sold when the boats return in the early evening. Alberto Zafrani is a wizard with fish, always inventing subtle new dishes. For the first course I find it hard to choose between tagliolini with prawns and radicchio and *spaghetti alla crema di scampi*. A really spectacular pasta dish is *spaghetti al cartoccio*. A sealed foil parcel is brought to the table and opened in front of the expectant audience, letting a mouthwatering garlic scented steam escape. Inside the silver packet is a delicious combination of pasta, tomatoes, white wine and mixed shellfish. The spaghetti has been partially cooked in the foil and become thoroughly impregnated with all the flavours. For the main course I would suggest a large fish to be shared between two. I usually choose a simply roasted *orata* (bream), *spigola* (sea bass) or *rombo* (halibut). There is a good wine list to complement these lovely fish, and the house wine by carafe is very pleasant.

In the warmer months tables are set outside in the courtyard and on cooler days the room inside is bright and cheerful.

Price: moderate; Amex, Diners, Visa
Closed: Thursday; part of August
Location: alongside jetty, Fiumicino, 28 km from Rome

~ RECIPE ~
Involtini ai Carciofi
Beef stuffed with artichokes from Cecchino dal 1887

8 thin slices of very lean beef (approx. 100 grms/4 oz each)
salt and black pepper
8 thin slices Parma ham (or other raw ham)
oil for frying
2 artichokes, with the coarse leaves and chokes removed
a little stock or half glass of white wine
400g/14 oz tin plum tomatoes

Season each slice of beef and cover with a slice of ham. Divide the cleaned artichokes in quarters. Place a quarter on each slice of beef and ham. Roll up each beef slice and secure with a toothpick. In a flame proof pan, heat the oil and fry for a few moments over a high flame. Cover with the chopped tomatoes and a little stock or white wine. Cook on a low flame for approximately 1½ hours. Remove sticks and serve. Serves 4.

Grottaferrata

*G*rottaferrata is one of the most charming of the Castelli towns with its spectacular early eleventh century abbey. On Monday morning a lively market is held in the piazza outside the abbey walls and a visit to the market can be followed by lunch at my favourite local trattoria.

Taverna dello Spuntino
Via Cicerone 22, Grottaferrata
Tel. 945 9366

'*Lo Spuntino*' started life as a wine *cantina* and under the restaurant, there are extensive wine cellars and a quaint fountain which can be ordered to spout the good local white wine. Today, Basilio Fontini, named after his grandfather the original owner, runs a lively trattoria which is warmly welcoming in the cooler months with its huge fireplace, old copper cooking pots and beautifully-arranged flowers. In summer, a few tables are set outside to enjoy the cool, perfumed evening breeze. The menu is very extensive and there is a lavish table of antipasti. Basilio's mother, Mirca, supervises the preparation of light home-made pasta. I particularly like the pasta with artichokes in which both appear in equal proportions. This area is famous for its succulent roast sucking pig, ' *maialino*', lamb and game in season, but there are many lighter dishes like the '*stracetti*' – tender pieces of veal topped with pungent rughetta (rocket or arugula) or other choice herbs and vegetables. The desserts are all homemade and there is a beautiful array of fruit, homely and exotic, which can be enjoyed with a glass of the interesting, slightly sweet, local red wine.

Price: Moderate; credit cards not accepted
Closed: Wednesday; end July first week August
Location: 21 km SE on the Via Appia

Anguillara Sabazia

Lake Bracciano, topped by its fairytale fourteenth century Orsini Castle, is only 32 kilometres from Rome and well worth a visit. (The castle is open to the public once a week: opening times should be checked in advance.) The lake is formed in the crater of an extinct volcano and three small towns have grown up around the lake: Bracciano, Trevignano and Anguillara. Bracciano has the castle, but there are better restaurants a few kilometres round the lake at Anguillara or Trevignano.

La Molaccia
Via San Biagio 2, Anguillara Sabazia
Tel. (06) 901 0356

In the medieval part of Anguillara, Antonietta and Bruno Polimeni have a tiny, intimate trattoria which they created from three storage caves cut in the rock. There are three tables in each of two of the small rooms, and in an even smaller carved grotto there are another two tables. Bruno comes from southern Calabria and Antonietta from northern Liguria – an interesting gastronomic union. The *pesto* we find on the menu in the summer and the fine olive oil from Oneglia reflect Antonietta's influence. She also chooses the very good wines. Bruno is the cook and the menu changes according to his mood and the fresh ingredients found in the market. He has a passion for rice and this explains the good risottos. His excellent pasta sauces include *pesto* in the summer and pappardelle with sausage in winter. As well as lake fish *persico* (perch) and *coregone* on Fridays, Bruno orders fish from the sea, and often makes *spaghetti con nero di seppie* (pasta cooked in cuttlefish ink which turns the spaghetti into a strange glistening black coil). The fish is usually cooked on the large charcoal grill and is excellent. Anguillara is believed to get its name from the plentiful supply of eels (*anguille*) in the lake, and Bruno prepares this local delicacy with great flair.

Bruno cooks accordingly to whim and his sweets reflect his mood. On a good day it is difficult to choose between apple pie, crème caramel and a parfait made with Strega liqueur.

Price: *moderate to inexpensive; credit cards not accepted*
Closed: *Monday; August*
Location: *32 km from Rome*

Viterbo

Viterbo, 81 kilometres north of Rome, is well worth a visit. It used to be an Etruscan stronghold, and during the Middle Ages it housed several popes. The city is still encircled by a massive stone wall and the medieval buildings are well-preserved. The most interesting quarter is San Pellegrino with its narrow cobbled streets and old Viterbese houses.

Il Richiastro
Via della Marrocca 16/18, Viterbo
Tel (0761) 223 609

Architects Giovanna and Cesare Scappucci opened *Il Richiastro* in 1981 because they felt that Viterbo should have a trattoria serving traditional local food in authentic suroundings. They lovingly restored the twelfth century buildings and the rooms have fine timbered ceilings.

The food is unusual because the Scappuccis have researched old, traditional recipes and employed a local housewife, Irma Segatori, to do the cooking rather than a professional chef.

Soups play an important role in Viterbo's culinary tradition so *Il Richiastro* serve at least four every day. I have fond memories of a good chestnut and lentil soup, and there are many unusual combinations of dried peas and beans, whole grains, and herbs and vegetables in season. Small portions of pasta follow, usually with mushrooms or *zucchine* sauces.

For the main course there is a choice of steak or, for bolder palates, more earthy recipes of tripe and offal. Among vegetables, I have enjoyed fennel with orange and a crisp combination of raw spinach leaves with mushrooms and shavings of parmesan cheese. The olive oil is very good, produced by the Scappucci themselves, and the wine in carafe is very pleasant.

Since the Scappuccis divide their time between architecture and the trattoria, *Il Richiastro* is only open from Thursday to Sunday inclusive. It is also closed at certain periods of the year, so it is essential to phone in advance.

Price: moderate; credit cards not accepted
Closed: Monday, Tuesday, Wednesday; August
Location: Viterbo, 81 km from Rome

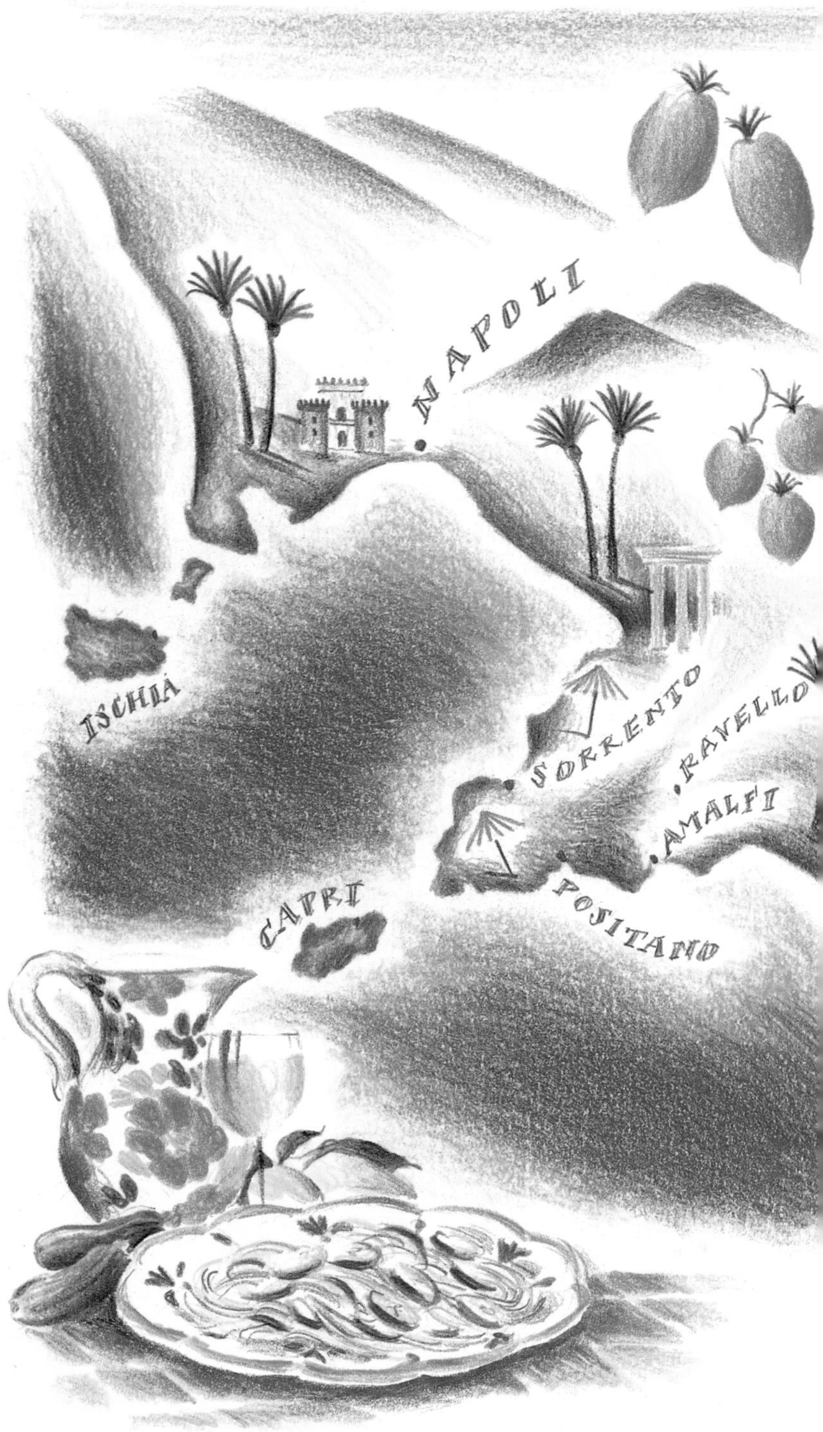
NAPOLI
ISCHIA
SORRENTO
RAVELLO
AMALFI
CAPRI
POSITANO

NAPLES
& the Amalfi Coast

*N*aples was once a great capital city, and everywhere you turn there are interesting reminders of her illustrious past. Naples has also been blessed by a smiling sea, a fertile soil and idyllic climate. These qualities have encouraged Neapolitans to base their cooking on good seafood, fresh vegetables and cheese. When the first commercial pasta factories were built around Naples, making use of the good local grain and taking advantage of the climate which is ideal for drying pasta, the people happily made this a vital part of their diet.

Traditional Neapolitan cooking has developed from a combination of *cucina povera* of the ordinary Neapolitans and the rich, complicated cooking of their rulers, largely influenced by centuries of French and Spanish domination. During these centuries of foreign rule, social conditions were grim and the locals had to struggle to survive. Their simple philosophy was *'O Francia o Spagna purché si magna'* – 'French or Spanish, it's all the same as long as we eat!'

Hunger was the great enemy and every simple meal was seen as a victory and a cause for celebration. The *cucina povera* uses great ingenuity to make simple ingredients festive. Comparatively expensive ingredients like cheese and eggs are used sparingly, with cheaper vegetables like potatoes and zucchini adding quantity. Many things from this tradition are fried because some of the poorest people had no homes and bought these snacks from street vendors.

The noble houses had French chefs called *monzù* – their version of *monsieur* – who created elaborate rich dishes based on French and Spanish traditions. However, the aristocratic houses were also devotees of the more humble pasta and pizza. Forks were invented to satisfy Ferdinand II's craving for pasta at state banquets, and Ferdinand IV had his pizza cooked in the furnace used to glaze the precious Capodimonte porcelain. After the unification of Italy, Pizza Margherita was named for the Queen of Savoy, the tomatoes, cheese and basil reflecting the red, white and green of the new flag's colours. Modern Neapolitans' love of good food is almost religious – their Christmas nativity scenes are full of market stalls and tables groaning with food – and the restaurants enjoy great scope as they roam freely through the recipes of both the 'poor' and 'noble' traditions.

Prices in Neapolitan restaurants and all along the beautiful Amalfi coast are very much influenced by whether the customer chooses to eat fish, always expensive, or not. Fish is nearly always served plainly grilled or baked in the oven, so that the fresh flavour is apparent.

Neapolitan pastry shops are famous for their great variety of cakes, and Neapolitan icecream is legendary. *"Gambrinus"*, perhaps the best of all the cafes specialising in icecream was founded in 1850, and is famous for its *spumone* (frothy-textured icecream with fruit and nuts), *coviglie*, sorbets and *granitas* made with lemon and coffee. Naples invented pizza, and visitors can also try the wide variety of traditional pizza at many informal pizzerias like *"Michele"*, via Cesare Sensale 3, or *"Ettore"*, via Santa Lucia 56. These are open morning and evening.

Climate and long years of Spanish influence have encouraged Neapolitans to eat late: lunch can start at 1.30-2.00 p.m. and dinner between 9.30 and 10.00 p.m. An invitation to come for drinks at 9.30 to be followed by dinner is very common.

Lastly, a word of advice. Naples has more than its fair share of petty criminals and it is best to avoid carrying a handbag or wearing gold jewellery in the streets. After dark, it is safer to keep to the well-lit and more populated main streets and take a radio taxi to and from the restaurant.

Il Pulcinella
Vico Ischitella 4, Naples
Tel. (081) 7642216

Il Pulcinella, two steps from the Riviera di Chiaia, near the sea front, is a small, quaint restaurant, almost a private dining club, where those in the know go to enjoy good Neapolitan home cooking. Signora Mussa, the owner, loves good food and over the years she has cooked happily for all her large family's celebrations. Now, with the help of her daughter, she gives customers her family recipes prepared with the same loving care. The daily set menu is planned according to 'how Mamma feels' and the produce in the market.

The service is friendly and the meal starts with a selection of tasty antipasti: *bruschetta* (garlic toast) topped with *zucchini* and *melanzane*, marrow (squash) flowers, potato croquettes, *zucchini scapece* and many other authentic starters. This is followed by one of Naples' traditional soups, such as *minestre maritata*, or pasta with lentils or chick peas. Or you might be given a good pasta with *ragù* or artichokes and peas. The fish or meat course follows the same mood of family cooking, and the desserts are simple but good. At Easter and Christmas the old, time-honoured recipes are used to make seasonal specialities.

Price: *Inexpensive; credit cards not accepted*
Closed: *Monday; August*
Location: *Mergerllina area, near the sea-front*

La Sacrestia
Via Orazo 116, Naples
Tel. (081) 664186

A long, winding road leads from the port up to the panoramic views and the beautiful terrace of La Sacrestia, which has won a position as one of Naples' top restaurants. It was opened in 1972 on Santa Lucia's day by Arnaldo Ponsiglione, and the menu reflects his passionate involvement with Neapolitan culinary traditions. He visited princely estates, religious institutions and ordinary households in search of authentic, time-honoured recipes, and borrowed freely from extravagant and simple kitchens alike, so that today, according to mood and pocket, you can choose the sumptuous *bucatini alla Principe di Napoli*, made with truffles, or the homely *pasta e ceci* made with chick peas.

Ponsiglione's son, Marco, values his gastronomic heritage but at the same time feels free to improvise, and the present menu is an interesting combination of the best of the old and the new.

There is a vast choice of antipasti and first courses. I love the black risotto made with squid – their ink turns the rice black – and the delicate pasta dishes that includes shrimps, artichokes and olives. The simply cooked fish is always superb, but this is also one of the few places which serves elaborate, inventive fish recipes.

Price: Expensive; Amex, Visa
Closed: Wednesday in general; August
Location: 10 minute taxi from centre

Ristorante Mimi alla Ferrovia
Via Alfonso D'Aragona 21, Naples
Tel. 081 5538525

The area around Naples' main train station is rather shabby and it is not a good idea to explore the back streets after dark. However, it would be a pity to miss a visit to Mimi alla Ferrovia (*ferrovia* means railway) near Piazza Garibaldi, particularly as radio taxis are safe and efficient.

This lively trattoria was started by the present owner's grandfather, who carefully sited his restaurant within easy reach of the good fish and vegetable markets of the old Porta Capuana and the busy central train station. 'Regulars' were soon attracted and today's customers are often grandchildren of the original diners, holding business lunches at the same tables where, as children, they wriggled impatiently through interminable family celebrations. The clientele is very varied: the world of sport is well represented, and professional and businessmen jostle family groups in pursuit of a table. The trattoria is always in demand so it is best to book in advance if possible.

The decor at Mimi alla Ferovia is completely unpretentious and although they have their share of celebrities this is a place where one goes to eat, drink and be merry, not to see and be seen. The bottles of wine adorning the room are within easy reach because they are there to be drunk. The large coloured bowls of live shellfish empty and fill with the steady rhythm of the tide as they get eaten and then replenished by fresh supplies from Terracina's fish market.

The owner produces his own wine in Lettere, south of Naples, a thin red wine that goes surprisingly well with fish. However, I usually order the dry white Libecchio from Sicily so admired by the artist Renato Guttuso, and then give the waiters free hand to bring the antipasti.

A series of small succulent treats are brought to the table a few at a time. Fresh mozzarella, stuffed fillets of sweet red peppers, pizza topped with the bitter green *scarole* (batavia) leaves, and then a selection of fried Neapolitan specialities: little fritters made from minute, new-born fish called *ceciniella*, small pastries or *panzerotti* filled with ricotta cheese and egg, various vegetables encased in crisp, puffy batter, and potato croquettes.

The selection of first courses is equally rich in variety and it is difficult to choose between the dense broths made with chick peas or beans and the mixed pasta – *ammiscata*, or the delicious pasta cooked in the oven or again the lavish linguine with scampi. Mimi also serves a superb fish soup which is a meal in itself.

The swordfish (*pesce spada*) is prepared very well. On my last visit I ate a small *spigola* – bass cooked simply in the oven. I think it had almost the best flavour of any fish I have ever eaten.

The traditional Neapolitan desserts make a fitting end to the meal, especially the *pastiera* made from grain and ricotta cheese and the rum baba.

Price: Moderate to expensive; Amex, Diners, Visa
Closed: Sunday
Location: Central Naples, near main railway station

La Cantinella
Via Nazario Sauro 23, Naples
Tel. (081) 404884

Giorgio Rosolino's La Cantinella is on the sea-front at Santa Lucia, but the small port, immortalized in the song, has disappeared.

La Cantinella, however, is admirable from any point of view. The atmosphere is calm and relaxed. The waiters are courteous and helpful and the food is uniformly good. The array of antipasti is dazzling. There are all the Neapolitan specialities, such as seafood fritters, stuffed pizzette, shellfish salad, vegetable *scapece* as well as the more expensive, sophisticated starters. It is tempting to make a meal of antipasti, but restraint is needed because the other courses are just as good. Try the deceptively simple *spaghetti alla vongole* or the opulent linguine with lobster (*aragosta*). Or if the asparagus is in season, indulge in the butterfly pasta, *farfalle con asparagi*.

The fish cooked simply in the oven – *al forno* – is always excellent, and *scampi al gratin* is hard to resist. I love the less expensive fish poached in *acqua pazza* – literally 'mad water' or water 'maddened', with olive oil, anchovy, bay leaves and chilli pepper. This restaurant is also a good place to sample salt cod (*baccalà*) cooked with tomatoes.

There is a good, intelligent wine list which is what one would expect from a restaurant called La Cantinella, which means a small *cantina* or wine cellar.

Price: Expensive; Amex, Diners, Visa
Closed: August, Sunday
Location: Santa Lucia seafront

ZUCCHINI CACIO E UOVA

Ristorante Ciro
Via Santa Brigida 71, Naples
Tel. 5524072

Ciro, in Santa Brigida, is one of my favourite Neapolitan restaurants. Near the Galleria Umberto arcade, it can easily be combined with a visit to the Royal Palace or San Carlo theatre. However, it is well worth crossing all Naples just to eat here if you are genuinely interested in Neapolitan gastronomy.

The Pace family used to own an old pizzeria and in 1932 Vicenzo and Ciro Pace decided to expand and move up-market to Via Santa Brigida. They retained the family tradition of good food at a fair price, and over the years Ciro has become a well-loved institution, with a widely varied clientele. Toscanini and Pirandello used to eat here and the menu has remained much the same. The atmosphere is plain and simple, but the welcome is warm. Expert waiters, like Lucio Prato, guide you through the large menu with consummate skill, referring constantly to Naples' culinary and cultural heritage. The menu is so extensive because Ciro caters for an enormous following of 'regulars'. Indeed, most of the customers are Neapolitans.

Begin by ordering the local white wine, Salopaca Masserie Venditti which is very enjoyable and good value for money. Then to the starters. *Zucchini cacio e uova* (see recipe) is delicious, made from baby marrows (squash), cheese and eggs. At one time it would have been a cheap, sustaining one-dish meal for a local family; today vegetarians could happily cook it for a main course. In spring, Ciro also serves a variation made with the very new

PIZZA MARGHERITA

zucchini and
their small flowers.

During these months, when the vegetables are so tender and delicious, you will also be offered pasta with peas and risotto with asparagus tips. My all-time favourite is *penne alla mozzarella e melanzane* (pasta with mozzarella cheese and aubergines (egg plants)). The *gattò di patate* (mashed potato cake) – a phonetic spelling of the French *gâteau* – is very good but filling so it is best to order one between several people. A similar dish is *sartù di riso* – an elaborate moulded rice concoction – but again it is a meal in itself, so don't order it unless you are very hungry.

For the main course you find excellent grilled meat and some traditional dishes like *spiedino di braciolette* (stuffed meat balls on a skewer) and veal *alla pizzaiola*. I particularly enjoy the fish and shellfish soup (*pignatiello e vavella*), which seems to have been influenced by the many years of Spanish domination. There is also a wide choice of vegetable dishes. The aromatic *scapece* way with vegetables is well worth sampling, and broccoli lovers should try the *friarelli*, a variety of broccoli which is only grown around Naples.

Ciro serves the usual desserts including the local *pastiera* made with ricotta cheese and raisins and cassata icecream.

Price: Moderate; Amex
Closed: Sunday, August
Location: Central Naples, near Galleria Umberto arcade

~ RECIPE ~
Zucchine Cacio e Uova
Zucchini, Egg and Cheese from Da Ciro, Naples

1 kg/2 lb small courgettes (zucchini), cut into strips
olive oil for frying
1 egg per person
50g/2 oz (½ cup) freshly grated Parmesan cheese
salt and freshly ground black pepper

Par-boil the courgette sticks for approximately 3 minutes and then drain. In a small frying pan, fry the courgettes in a little olive oil. Lightly beat the eggs together and add the Parmesan cheese. Pour into the frying pan with the courgettes. Season with salt, stir and remove from the heat just before the eggs amalgamate. Season with black pepper and serve immediately. Serves 4.

Amici Miei
Via Monte di Dio 78, Naples
Tel. (081) 405727

Amici Miei is a small, dark restaurant where traditional Neapolitan dishes are served to an appreciative regular clientele. The building, which orginally formed part of the Baracco family estate, was left to the family cook, Concetta, in gratitude for the many memorable meals she had prepared. She opened a restaurant called, Chez Concetta, and served the same dishes to her customers who soon became regulars. Although, inevitably with the passing years, the restaurant has changed hands, the style of cooking remains the same.

Little fried nibbles are brought to the table with the water and wine. I enjoyed an interesting dry, sparkling red wine – Gragnano – which is produced near Salerno. This is one of the few restaurants where it can be found.

The traditional pasta dishes include pasta and *fagioli* (beans), famous throughout Naples, penne with *melanzane* (aubergines/ eggplant and mozzarella cheese) and the extravagant *Carnevale lasagne* with its very rich filling intended to warm the memory through the Lenten fast. The second courses range from the homely sausage and *friarielli* (broccoli) to the more ubiquitous steak or *carpaccio* (thinly sliced raw beef). The desserts are all home-made and the fruit tart is very popular.

Price: Moderate; Amex, Diners
Closed: Monday, Sunday eve; August
Location: Mergellina area.

La Fazenda
Calcata Marechiaro 58, Naples
Tel. (081) 7697420

La Fazenda is the ideal place for a long, tranquil, romantic meal (as long as you do not go on a Sunday or public holiday). The restaurant is situated on a hill high above the part of the coast known as Marechiaro, meaning 'transparent sea'.

La Fazenda means a large agricultural estate and, although here the dimensions are more modest, most of the vegetables served are home-grown. Two of my favourite pasta dishes make excellent use of the fresh vegetables – *penne* with sweet peppers, aubergines/eggplant and mozzarella cheese, and *orecchiette* cooked with green, leafy vegetables.

The chicken and rabbit are home-produced and very good cooked in the tangy huntsman style – *alla cacciatora*. The choice of fish depends on what the local Marechiaro fishermen have caught that day. It is cooked very simply to preserve its natural flavour.

Price: Moderate to expensive
Closed: Sunday, August 10–25
Location: On the coast, kilometres from centre

Giuseppone a Mare
Via Ferdinando Russo 3, Naples
Tel. (081) 7696002

In a beautiful position, right down on the sea front in the district of Posillipo, this restaurant opened in 1889 as a simple eating-place for the local fishermen. Over the years, it has become a Neapolitan institution – large, impersonal and, at times, inefficient. On one recent visit my *linguine al scampi* was good but my companions complained that their *risotto alla pescatore* (fisherman's risotto) suggested that the fisherman had had a poor catch that day!

Having said all this, I must admit that I found the lunch enjoyable! The wine – Greco di Tufo – was good and the fish was fresh. Moreover, the setting is a perpetual joy. This small, tranquil inlet with its blue sea, painted houses and distant views of Vesuvius conjures up a vision of Naples of a hundred years ago.

Price: Expensive; Amex, Diners, Visa
Closed: Sunday, Christmas
Location: 8 kilometres west of central Naples

Rosiello
Via S. Strato 10, Posillipo, Naples

In springtime Rosiello is probably the prettiest restaurant in Naples. Capo Posillipo on the coast was loved by the ancient Greeks and Romans for its calm beauty, and its name comes from the Greek, *pausilypon* – a place to ease all pain. Sitting on the terrace under the thick forty-year old wisteria and looking down at the sea is instantly soothing. When the food starts to arrive the feeling of well-being expands rapidly.

The Concetta family who own the restaurant have been running country trattorias for four generations, and they produce their own vegetables, olive oil and wine.

The fish is supplied by a local fisherman so the menu changes according to the catch, and it is usually cooked very simply in the oven or on the grill. Grilled large prawns and small squid are particularly good. I made a delightful gastronomic discovery here. One of the specialities is *polipo affogato* (drowned octopus) and, though I was a little put off by the name, I tried it – the taste

was out of this world. Small octopus is stewed with tomatoes and black olives in an individual casserole and the subtle combination of flavours makes it a highly memorable dish. There is a good selection of fresh fruit sorbets to finish the meal.

Throughout the meal, I drank the owner's own wine – a thin dry red – and it went very well with everything, even the fish.

Price: *Moderate to expensive; Amex*
Closed: *Wednesday, August 10 – 20*
Location: *Posillipo area*

Sorrento

*A*lthough Sorrento has been adversely affected by mass tourism it would be a mistake to dismiss it out of hand. The old hotels high on the cliffs have superb views from their balconies and their lush gardens are perfumed with long-established wisteria, jasmine and bourgainvillaea. Moreover, there are three restaurants in the near vicinity which are worth a visit.

'O Parrucchiano
Corso Italia 71, Sorrento
Tel. (081) 878321

In summer, Corso Italia is thronged with restless visitors in search of imported beer or tea-rooms. They seem to pass by 'O Parrucchiano without a second glance and, indeed, from the outside it is difficult to imagine the delights within. The restaurant has a series of beautiful terraced gardens, and it is best to ignore the tables in the first room and climb up the central staircase to the splendours above.

The trattoria was opened in 1890 by an ex-seminarian and it quickly became known to the locals as 'the priest's place' or, in dialect 'O Parrucchiano'. It has been run by the same family for three generations, and today Enzo Manniello continues the tradition of good local food. The chef, Antonio Mascalo, comes from nearby Sant'Agata and has been working here for over 25 years.

All the traditional pasta dishes are served including pasta *alla sorrentina* (with tomato and melted mozzarella cheese). The pizza is very good as well and almost a complete meal. Main courses follow the Neapolitan tradition of simply-prepared fish, more elaborate meat dishes and excellent fresh vegetables.

There is a good choice of Italian wines and a rather pungent local wine served by the jug.

The local oranges, lemons and walnuts are used in the desserts, and there are very delicate profiteroles filled with lemon cream.

Price: *Moderate; credit cards not accepted*
Closed: *Wednesday from November to May*
Location: *Central Sorrento*

Maria Grazia
Spiaggia Marina del Cantone, Nerano
Tel. (081) 8081209

Marina del Cantone is a small fishing village 12 kilometres from Sorrento along a narrow, winding road. The scenery is beautiful and the island of Capri can be seen looming out of the sea surprisingly close at hand. Many of the *Maria Grazia* customers come by yacht, motor boat or hired rowing boat. Lunch is the time to come when visitors sit around in swimsuits on the shady terrace on the beach.

This deceptively simple trattoria has been owned by the Mellino family for generations. There is no menu because the customers come with the sole purpose of eating the specialities. The *antipasti* are fresh anchovy fillets, stuffed sweet peppers, fresh mozzarella, potato croquettes and huge, crisply fried marrow (squash) flowers. Their famous pasta speciality, *spaghetti alla Maria Grazia*, is made with *zucchini*. It has to be one of the most delicious pasta recipes ever invented, and most regulars regard it as the high spot of the meal. The kitchen is kept steadily busy preparing fresh batches and unfed customers watch with greedy eyes as each huge, steaming bowl is carried out to Salvatore, the boss, for the final stir before servings are portioned out.

The next course, fresh fish, is almost an anticlimax after such delicious beginnings. Now for the first time orders vary. Depending on the local catch, there is fish cooked simply in the oven, grilled fish or a mixture of fried prawns, squid and tiny fish.

The meal usually ends with a jug of white wine filled with sliced peaches, if peaches are in season, or a bowl of mixed fresh fruit.

Price: *Moderate to expensive; credit cards not accepted*
Closed: *One month in winter*
Location: *On the beach, 12 kilometres from Sorrento*

Don Alfonso 1890
Piazza Sant'Agata, Sant'Agata sui Due Golfi
Tel. (081) 8780026

Sant'Agata is 9 kilometres from Sorrento and in this little village, set high on the coast, is one of the finest restaurants – certainly the finest cellar – in this region of Italy. Alfonso Iaccarino's family have been hoteliers for five generations – his great-grandmother had a small hotel here in Sant'Agata. He trained at the hotel school in Stresa with the idea of following the family tradition, but he gradually discovered that he was more interested in good food and wine. With his wife, Livia, he has developed this interest until it has become a ruling passion. Although they have travelled widely in Italy and France studying new techniques and enlarging their repertoire, they have not lost contact with regional culinary traditions. They continue to make good use of local ingredients and many traditional recipes are magically transformed so that they become lighter and healthier. Other recipes are delightfully new, invented with flair and imagination.

There are three menus to choose from – a short, yet complete, traditional local menu; a more elaborate 'tasting' menu, designed to give a good introduction to the Don Alfonso style of cooking;

ON ALFONSO

and an exciting daily menu that varies according to the best fresh ingredients available.

My favourite starters are rolled fillets of *dentice* (a warm-water white fish) served with rocket (arugula) leaves and fennel seeds, and a sort of quenelle made with *boccadoro* (a fish like sea bass, literally 'golden mouth') served with a carrot sauce. For those who like sweet-savoury combinations there is an unusual foie gras pastry with an orange-flavoured honey sauce.

The pasta dishes are all so delicious it is difficult to choose. Inspired by local traditions, tagliolini is dressed with a sharp shrimp, orange and lemon sauce. Local mozzarella and tomatoes are transformed into a delicate souffle creation. I particularly enjoyed tiny light cannelloni filled with fresh asparagus and truffles.

An enticing main dish of fish with watercress and pistachio nuts is offered, and fried shrimps and squid are given a novel twist by the addition of an artichoke and fresh garlic sauce. This is one of the few southern restaurants to serve first-class lamb among its good range of meat dishes.

The desserts made here are deliciously different and served with a fine sense of fantasy. First, the elegant white plates are decorated with a series of cassis cream arabesques. Then among the swirls there is a mouth-watering selection of delights including a bavarian cream made with local citrus fruits, the traditional baba revolutionised by fresh raspberries, and a sculpted crystalline strawberry sweet fit for a Snow Queen.

For years Alfonso and Livia have spent every holiday touring the great vineyards of Europe and a superb wine cellar has been built up with great professional skill. However, when you talk to the Iaccarinos you realise the love and care behind this expertise. The wine almost seems a member of the family as it is admired and caressed then tenderly put back into place. There is a good collection of *grappa*, whisky and other more homely liqueurs and some outstanding olive oil. Don Alfonso produces and bottles his own olive oil at 'La Peracciole' in nearby Torca.

The decoration of the restaurant is light and attractive with its graceful silver place settings and fine glasses. There are even a few bedrooms furnished with the same discerning eye and attention to detail, where one or two fortunate beings can prolong their encounter with the Iaccarino's splendid hospitality.

Price: Expensive; Amex, Diners, Visa
Closed: From January 7 to February 26, Sunday evening and Monday
Location: 9 kilometres south of Sorrento

Positano

Positano is as fascinating today as it was when it was first 'discovered', but it has been 'discovered' many times. Myriads of famous people through the ages have been enchanted and it is easy to believe that Ulysses' Sirens really lurk in the waters of this little port. Positano is such a feast for the eyes that food seems to take second place until appetising aromas drift up from the trattorias on the beach.

Chez Black
Tel. (089) 875036

Chez Black is owned by Salvatore Russo. Back in the Sixties, his deep suntan earned him the nickname 'Black' among English visitors, and Salvatore re-christened the family restaurant to give it an international slant. Happily the cooking remains one hundred percent Italian. My favourite dish is *linguine agli scampi*: at *Chez Black* this lavish pasta feast is a complete meal in itself. When I ate there recently my greed and enjoyment were so obvious that several tables of tourists ordered their lunch by pointing at me!

The house speciality is *linguine all'aragosta*. The lobsters are small and tasty and kept specifically for this dish which must be ordered the day before. Only one table a day is served with this delicacy so it becomes a sort of gastronomic status symbol, presented with a great flourish. Minute heart-shaped pizzas decorate the borders of the plate, absorbing some of the delectable sauce, and these are regarded as a great treat.

All the pizzas here are very good. They are served at lunch and dinner with many different toppings. *Pizza alla Black* is unusual because it contains no cheese. The rich selection of shellfish is held to the pizza crust by the tomatoes.

The refreshing finish to the meal is a sharp salad made with fresh tropical fruit. Salvatore offers favoured guests a glass of his home-made lemon liqueur (see recipe) – delicious, but since it is 95 per cent proof, it could prove lethal for those setting off on the famous Amalfi drive with its narrow hairpin bends!

Price: Moderate; Amex, Diners, Visa
Closed: January 10 – February 28
Location: Sea-front

Amalfi

Amalfi was once a great maritime republic rivalling Venice and Genoa. Her fame was such that in the early 17th century, the English playwright, Webster, set his 'Duchess of Malfi' here. Today Amalfi is a small resort famous for the Emerald Grotto and beautiful dimpled lemons.

~ RECIPE ~
Liquore di Limone
Lemon Liqueur from Chez Black, Positano

100 g/3½ oz pared lemon zest
1 litre/1¾ pints (1 quart) 95% proof pure alcohol
330g/11 oz (1⅔ cups) liquid sugar (cane sugar or ordinary sugar)
1 litre/1¾ pints (1 quart) water

Mix the lemon zest into the alcohol or vodka and leave for 2 weeks. Filter the liquid after this time, then add the sugar and water and bottle. Leave for at least 1 week before drinking.

Cantina di Zaccaria
Via S. Quasimodo, Amalfi
Tel. (089) 871807

On the extreme east of the Amalfi bay, past the old Saracen tower, some two kilometres from the town centre, there is a small trattoria perched on the cliff with a stupendous view. It takes some finding but just before the tunnel, turn into the small road to the right. For full effect, book an outside table for lunch or an early dinner to enjoy the sunset.

This family-run trattoria serves very good fish and for the first course there is an ample *sauté di frutti di mare* – a large selection of shellfish tossed in a pan with garlic, olive oil, lemon juice, parsley and a sprinkle of white wine. The local white wine, Greco di Tufo, goes very well with this as you sit back to admire the view. Among the pasta dishes there is delectable *linguine agli scampi* (long noodles with scampi) and *pasta e fagioli con le vongole* (pasta with beans and clams). The grilled mixed fish is succulent, and the *fritto mistro di mare* (mixed fried seafood) light and crisp. The fish varies according to the catch but it is always fresh and well-prepared.

Price: Moderate; credit cards not accepted
Closed: Monday
Location: 2 kilometres east of Amalfi at Atrani

Gemma
Via Cavalieri di Malta, Amalfi
Tel. (089) 871345

Gemma is a simple, family-run trattoria very near the cathedral, reached up a flight of steps and a narrow alley off the main shopping street. In the warmer months it is possible to sit outside on the terrace and sample the local specialities. *Zuppa di pesce* (fish soup) is full of flavour and almost a meal in itself, and linguine with scampi or pasta stuffed with ricotta cheese are both good starters. For the main dish, there is a choice of fish of every shape and size and some appealing dishes of mixed vegetables fried in batter. The desserts are home-made, and I enjoyed the *crostata di limone* (lemon tart).

Price: Inexpensive; credit cards not accepted
Closed: January 10-February 28
Location: Central Amalfi

Ravello

A few kilometres outside Amalfi a steep, winding road leads up through vineyards and olive groves to cool, peaceful Ravello, which hangs like a balcony over the Salerno coast.

The Duomo and Villa Rufolo date from its prosperity in the eleventh century. In the last century, Wagner wrote part of his opera 'Parsifal' here.

Cumpa Cosima
Via Roma, Ravello
Tel. (089) 857156

You cannot eat outside in this family-run trattoria but you do get a memorable meal. Netta Bottone serves good, traditional food making intelligent use of all her many local resources. The trattoria is patronised by the locals and no concessions are made to tourist tastes, but Netta is always very willing to bring small portions of different pasta dishes, so that visitors can try out the variety. Her trattoria is almost self-sufficient: the pasta is home-made and the meat comes from the butcher shop next door, still run by Netta's father, Cosimo. The vegetables are all home-grown and picked at just the right moment. The delicious *salame* and *caciotta* cheese are made by Netta and her family, and they produce their own olive oil and wine.

Netta uses many old family recipes and places great importance on top quality ingredients. She takes full advantage of the family butcher shop and the menu changes according to season.

If you arrive in spring be sure to try her artichokes baked in layers with Parmesan cheese. The home-made desserts use seasonal fruits, and the icecream here is very good.

Netta is full of enthusiasm and loves to talk about her work. She knows all the old local traditions and I was fascinated when she explained to me that wine must only be filtered when there is a new moon in April! Listen to her suggestions and enjoy all the good things she will spread before you. She is a lavish host.

Price: Inexpensive; Amex, Diners, Visa
Closed: Monday, from November to March
Location: Central Ravello

Capri

Capri is still enchanting but how I envy the Roman Emperors, Augustus and Tiberius, who were able to enjoy the natural beauty of the island without all the artificial *dolce vita* of today. This is a fashionable spot where it pays to be a little wary. Reserve tables at a chosen restaurant well in advance.

La Capannina
Via della Botteghe, 14, Capri
Tel. (081) 8370732

One of my favourite restaurants in Capri, *La Capannina*, is blessed with a cool courtyard where you can eat in hot weather. Antonio De Angelis never fails to give every guest a warm welcome, and the service is impeccable even when the restaurant is very busy. Antonio has a good selection of wines, but for years he has been pioneering to secure some recognition for the local Capri white wine. Even in the recent past every small landowner made his own wine and the results were very inconsistent, but in the last two years a wine-making cooperative has been set up with stringent quality control and the results are very much more pleasing. So, a good start to the meal is a bottle of Capri white wine.

Antonio presents a general menu plus a fairly long list of daily specialities. The salad of crab, shrimps and rocket *(arugula)* is very good, and I love the unusual dish of fillets of aubergine (eggplant) rolled and stuffed with ricotta cheese *(melanzane alla monachina)*. This is a good place to try *ravioli alla caprese*, a local speciality in which the ravioli is stuffed with cheese and then fried. For a lighter pasta dish, try *linguine al sugo di scorfano*. The *scorfano* is the ugly red fish which gives such a good flavour to mediterranean fish soups. In the spring *La Capannina* also does a good dish of pasta with marrow (squash) flowers. There is a very wide choice of fish and meat main dishes or you can allow yourself to be tempted by a dish of fried *zucchini* and mozzarella. The mozzarella comes from the mainland town of Massalu-brense which is famous for its good plaits *(treccia)* of genuine mozzarella made from buffalo's milk.

Price: Moderate; Amex, Visa
Closed: Wednesday, November to March
Location: Central Capri, near Piazza Umberto

La Pigna
Via Lo Palazzo 30, Capri
Tel. (081) 8370280

This is a favourite haunt that I have returned to many times and it is an ideal choice for a romantic summer evening. The eating area is surrounded by flowering plants and trees and the skilfull lighting makes the garden a magic grove at night glowing with subtle colour.

Renato De Gregorio places great importance on good local produce and provides a constantly changing menu. The best plan is to be advised by Renato himself who is constantly searching old forgotten recipes to bring variety and health to his cooking and he will plan an exciting meal. When I was there recently I tried linguine flavoured with oil and rosemary and pasta with *zucchini*. Both were very good. The fish dishes are consistently good with some unusual combinations, and there is rabbit and chicken for those who prefer a low-fat meat. There are unusual, interesting desserts, and the meal can be rounded off with a glass of Renato's home-made liqueur.

Price: Moderate to expensive; Amex, Visa
Closed: Tuesday, except July to September; November to March
Location: Central Capri

Anacapri

*A*nacapri, the highest part of the island of Capri, is reached by a breathtaking road and, as you round the final bend a statue of the Emperor Augustus seems to be raising his hand in welcome. Anacapri is quieter than Capri itself but is easily reached by the frequent buses and taxis making the five-minute journey up and down the hill.

Nello al Faro
Località Punta Carena
Tel. (081) 837 1798

From Anacapri it is a short bus or taxi ride to this trattoria carved out of the rocks right near the lighthouse. There are no other buildings in this isolated spot, and Nello once had to rebuild after an exceptionally rough sea destroyed his establishment. Even on a calm day, the sea pounds endlessly against the rocks and it is often difficult to negotiate the iron ladder to get back to dry land after your swim. There are deck chairs and changing rooms just below the trattoria so it is easy to be tempted to have a swim before the meal. In the off-season months *Nello's* is open only for lunch but in the warmer months he is open late into the night.

As one would expect from this setting the emphasis is on good fresh fish cooked very simply. However, there are interesting pasta dishes with vegetable sauces, and I recommend the pasta with aubergine (eggplant) and mozzarella.

Price: Inexpensive; credit cards not accepted
Closed: One month in winter
Location: Seafront

Ischia

*T*he largest island in the bay of Naples, Ischia is known for its volcanic nature and numerous thermal springs, as well as lush vegetation and little ports.

Girasole
Spiaggia Fumarole, Sant'Angelo
Tel. (9081) 999297

This restaurant can only be reached by boat, and gives one a chance to escape the summer crowds. Since it is part of a complex including hot volcanic sands and a sauna, a refreshing swim and good food can be preceded by a therapy session which does wonders for aching bones. A three-wheeler taxi will take you to Sant'Angelo, and the *Girasole* is 10 minutes by water taxi.

The atmosphere at *Girasole* is always calm and unhurried. All the most prized fish is available but the more simple house specialities are really memorable, such as a simple spaghetti dressed with good olive oil, parsley and finely chopped, creamy coloured garlic. Light, lemon-flavoured meat balls, chopped squash flowers fried in a yeast batter, crisp croquettes filled with creamy potatoes, and a fresh green leafy vegetable follow, or you can try boned fresh anchovies filled with mozzarella cheese and then fried. The meal finishes with good fresh fruit.

Price: Moderate to expensive; credit cards not accepted
Closed: Mid-October to mid-March
Location: Ten minutes by water-taxi from Sant'Angelo

'O Padrone D' O'Mare
Via Circumvallazione 4, Lacco Ameno
Tel. (081) 986159

This relaxed, unpretentious restaurant and pizzeria is well off the tourist circuit although it enjoys a superb location on the water's edge, near the luxury Regina Isabella hotel. It is run by four brothers who are busy with the tables while their wives, sister and aunt do the cooking. On the ground floor Ciro presides over the pizzas which can be eaten on the cool terrace surrounded by small boats bobbing about on their moorings. Upstairs are the dining-room and large terrace facing the sea where the serious eating is done. Although all the usual seafood pasta dishes are served here, the local people come to enjoy the great *zuppa di pesce* (fish soup), the house speciality. The zuppa is a substantial one-course meal: and it is so rich in fish it is served on a huge flat platter, not in a bowl. All it needs is bread to mop up some of the exquisite sauce.

There is a short wine list, but the house wine served in cool pottery jugs is very pleasant ahd highly recommended.

Price: Inexpensive; credit cards not accepted
Closed: Tuesday; mid-November to mid-February
Location: Sea front, Lacco Ameno

BARI
POLIGNANO
MONOPOLI
BRINDISI
ALBEROBELLO
LECCE
OTRANTO
CASTRO
TRICASE

LECCE,
Puglia & the Heel of Italy

*L*ecce, capital of the unspoiled Salento peninsular, is an unusual city full of contradictions. Sometimes called 'the queen of the Baroque', Lecce contains many beautiful churches built from the local soft, yellow limestone, *pietra leccese* which lends itself to intricate carving. Foreign rulers of Puglia favoured Lecce. The Roman Emperor, Hadrian, built a good road linking the city to the important port of Brindisi, and excavations this century unearthed a magnificent amphitheatre seating 25,000 spectators. When Naples was the capital of the kingdom of the Two Sicilies, Lecce enjoyed its proximity to the Court, adopting many Spanish customs. The unification of Italy was a bitter blow. Although it meant the end of foreign rule, Lecce was now some 600 kilometres from the spiritual, temporal and geographical centre and even today this isolation is very real.

Yet this elegant, worldly city, through its very inaccessibility, has preserved many traditions that have been lost elsewhere. Since the economy has always been agricultural (comparative prosperity originated from the profitable tobacco crop) the culinary traditions are based on grain, olive oil, vegetables, fruit and wine. The healthy food of Puglia is what modern dieticians have come to recognise as ideal. Meat has never played an important part in the local diet, though in the cooler months horsemeat and several lamb specialities are prepared. *Gnemeriedde*, made from stuffed lamb's intestine, is a dish found all over the region under many different names, some of them licentious, and shows a very clear Greek influence. Around Lecce there were several Greek settlements, with one small town even called 'Calimera', 'good-morning' in Greek and several localities still use a dialect form known as 'griko'. The rocky coastline and the deep blue of the sea evoke the feeling of Greece as it was before the days of mass tourism.

The regional cheeses of Puglia are very good, including several forms of ricotta like the stronger *caccioricotta* and the spring *ricotta marzolina*. Puglia is famous for its mozzarella and *burrata*, a delicious form enriched with cream and wrapped in green leaves.

The ever-present sea provides the basis for a wealth of fish dishes ranging from extravagant lobster to simple stuffed mussels, *cozze arraganate*. Red mullet, *triglie*, are prized around the Castro coast and there are many different fish soups, including one version believed to have originated in Sparta.

The bread down here is superb and local bakers often use traditional wood ovens to bake great crusty loaves in many shapes. Each area has its own stuffed bread such as *puddica* made with tomatoes and garlic and *puccia* stuffed with black olives. Hard twisted breadsticks, *turallini*, flavoured with fennel seeds or chillies are usually served at the beginning of a meal, and often dipped into the wine. *Friselle*, square or round, once eaten in times of dire need as a complete meal, are made from whole-wheat flour or oatmeal and baked until they are very hard so that they will keep. Dipped in water to soften them slightly, they are eaten with masses of olive oil and chopped tomatoes. At sea, fishermen even dip them overboard to get water and salt together. Today they sometimes appear as antipasti.

In Puglia, pasta is very important, and the many different forms include *orecchiette* (little ears) which change size according to the area. Since women always helped on the land, the local pasta sauces are usually quickly made from fresh vegetables and olive oil. Lecce has its own antique dish loved by the poet Horace, *ciceri e tria*, chick peas with a mixture of boiled and crisply fried pasta. As well as the endless combinations of pasta and vegetables, Puglia boasts unusual soups that use artichokes, wild asparagus, fennel, sweet peppers, *melanzane* (aubergine/eggplant) and *rughetta* (rocket/aragula). A speciality is a dish of pureéd dried broad (fave) beans and *cicoria*, bitter greens, rather like sorrel.

Vegetables in Puglia are preserved in an infinite number of ways to add to the rich array of antipasti, such as red tomatoes dried in the sun and preserved in olive oil. Small fried stuffed pastries, *panzerotti*, are made with a variety of fillings. One Lecce speciality is a form of *panzerotti* made from rice. Rice is unusual in Puglia except in a *tiella* or *tiedde*, a dish found throughout the region, made from layers of rice, potatoes and mussels baked in an earthenware dish.

Raw vegetables are often served in this region at the end of a meal instead of fruit. Huge platters of tender celery and fennel are brought to the table to aid the digestion. However, the fruit here is really superb and, if they are in season, it would be a pity to miss the figs, prickly pears or watermelons. Traditional desserts use almonds and quince and there is a sweet version of the fritters called *pèttole*. Lecce has a strange sounding sweet made with pigs' blood and brains, the legendary *sanguinaccio*.

In the past, Pugliese wines have been sent north to be blended with those from other regions. In the last few years, however, Puglia has been cutting the quantity of wine produced in order to raise the quality. Leone de Castris started to produce quality wines before the Second World War, including a strong rosé, 'Five Roses', and a light, tingling white, 'Ursi'. Their new Chardonnay is very pleasant and the Salice Salentino is a good robust red. I find some of the other rosé wines a little insipid but any white Locorotondo is usually a safe bet.

In the great heat of the south, mealtimes always get later and later. Lunch is not served much before 1.30 and dinner can begin as late as 9 p.m., or 10 or even 11 p.m.

Visitors should take care of their possessions, especially in ports like Bari, and avoid wearing valuable jewellery in the streets.

Gambrinus Hotel Patria

Piazzette Riccardi 13, Lecce
Tel. (0832) 29431

The Hotel Patria is an historic hotel dating from the beginning of the last century and its facade echoes the famous Santa Croce church nearby. Although the hotel is a little tired in appearance, the dining room is run very successfully as an independent restaurant by Marcello de Santis who started his career here as a kitchen boy. The Murano wall lights and the graceful large central window, nearly a hundred years old, are the only hint of a forgotten era in this modern efficient restaurant.

The main attractions of *Gambrinus* now are the good

traditional food and Marcello's unassuming professional expertise. A rich array of antipasti and hot, mouth-watering nibbles are brought out sizzling from the kitchen to every table. All the traditional pasta and vegetable dishes can be found here, and the main course selection offers a wide choice of meat dishes and good, fresh fish prepared very simply in the local manner. The dessert trolley has varied delights and Marcello keeps a good wine cellar. Ask him to choose an interesting bottle for you to try.

Price: Inexpensive; Amex, Visa
Closed: Sunday; August; Christmas
Location: central Lecce, near Santa Croce church

Ristorante Plaza
Via 140 Rgt. Fanteria 12, Lecce
Tel. (0832) 25093

In 1955 Italo Carico opened his restaurant conveniently placed near Piazza Mazzini and the commercial centre. His wife, Anna, and other members of the family, help him to provide a daily feast of local dishes in a simple, unpretentious setting.

A wide array of typical vegetable antipasti, as well as plates of tiny mozzarella, small potato croquettes and delicious *panzerotti* are brought as starters. The pasta course nearly always includes *tubettini alle cozze* – short pasta tubes with mussels, *orecchiette a rape* – ear-shaped pasta with turnip tops, *taiedda alla leccese* (rice and mussels) and the delicious *ciceri e tria*. The second course offers a fair choice of dishes prepared to order, such as swordfish steaks and assorted grilled meats on skewers. The desserts are simple, there is plenty of good local fruit and the house wine is very pleasant.

Price: *Inexpensive; credit cards not accepted*
Closed: *Sundays; August*
Location: *central Lecce, near Piazza Mazzini*

Carlo V
Via Palmieri 45, Lecce
Tel. (0832) 45151

This elegant restaurant is in one of the most famous streets of old Lecce, very near the *duomo* and the imperial Triumphal Arch. The cross vaulted ceiling glows in the evening candlelight and the young chefs prepare 'new' dishes for fashionable Lecce. However, traditional dishes are also available and you find *zuppa di orzo* (barley soup) and stuffed filet of horsemeat side by side with *carpaccio* of swordfish and other innovations. The home-made desserts contain many traditional delights, like the almond and caramel *cupeta*. There is a good choice of regional and national wines.

Price: *Moderate; Amex, Visa*
Closed: *Monday; August*
Location: *central Lecce, near the cathedral*

Il Satirello

Localita Torre Chianca, Lecce
Tel (0832) 656121

The old white-washed *masserie* are one of the distinctive features of the Pugliese countryside – large, often ornate homesteads and outbuildings, frequently surrounded by a defensive wall to keep out marauding pirates from the coast. In 1955, Franco and Franca Alvino, already involved in the family's famous café and pastry shop in central Lecce, decided to convert their old *masseria*, by now engulfed on the edge of town, into a restaurant. The original eighteenth century structure with its small church, olive press and numerous outbuildings, is now transformed into an attractive combination of courtyard and dining-room.

While you are studying the menu, a plate of hot crisp *pèttole* (a Leccese speciality made from deep-fried yeast dough) is brought to the table. The antipasti trolley is full of appetising preparations of *zucchine*, artichokes, sweet peppers, *melanzane* (aubergine/eggplant), mussels and small, tender octopus (*pulperizze*). Small portions of *taiedde* (rice and mussels) and *fave e cicoria* can be tried before going on to the pasta. Specialities include *tubetti al sugo de cernia*, short pasta tubes in a fish sauce, and *gnocchetti verdi* made from spinach, potatoes, eggs and cheese. For the main course there is plainly grilled lamb, kid and good beef or fresh fish supplied by four local fishing boats. In season, game and wild boar are on the menu. Since there is a *pasticceria* (pastry shop) in the family there are always good desserts as well as great platters of luscious Pugliese fruit. The wine list includes the best regional wines and some good national bottles.

Price: Moderate; Amex, Visa
Closed: Tuesday; part of July
Location: 9 km from central Lecce

Otranto

*O*tranto is famous for the bravery it showed in 1480 when it resisted the mighty Turkish fleet, throwing the keys of the city into the sea in a defiant refusal to surrender. Eight hundred civilians were eventually massacred. The town's fortifications were reinforced after this attack and today the port is dominated by the fifteenth century Aragonese castle.

Il Duca d'Aragona
Via Scupoli 32, Otranto
Tel. (0836) 86165

This elegantly austere restaurant is reached by a series of narrow alleys and steps running up from the port to the old town. The building is old and feels like a private house. While you are waiting for your table one of the politely attentive sons of the house offers you an *aperitivo* then leads you through to the dining-rooms which look out past the walls to the harbour and open sea.

The restaurant was opened in the early summer of 1988 by a local-born banker, Mario Morray, and his wife, Natalia. Mario chooses the fish personally in the market before starting work at the bank, and the two sons, still at school, double as waiters.

A good selection of regional wines vouches for Natalia's respect for local culinary traditions, and a great table set in the hallway displays a rich selection of local fish, vegetables and pastry antipasti. Although summer visitors often seem to prefer seafood, Natalia continues to prepare some traditional dishes

every day such as the *orecchiette* served with a leafy green vegetable. Otranto specialities include *cefalo arrosto* (baked grey mullet), eels from the nearby Alimin lakes, and *cupiddi*, small fish first fried then marinated in saffron and vinegar. To finish the meal most customers seem happy with icecream served with a sauce of Natalia's homemade jam or perhaps a simple fruit tart.

Price: Moderate; credit cards not accepted
Closed: Wednesday
Location: 41 km from Lecce, in the old town

Castro

*C*astro Alta, the village on the cliff, is made up of narrow little streets with simple houses white-washed or painted in shades of blue, pink and green, often draped with fishing nets stretched out to dry. Time seems to have stopped in the hot afternoons when old ladies swathed in black bring out their hard kitchen chairs to sit silently in the shady streets. A winding road leads down to Castro marina whose small, deep, natural harbour has proved irresistible over the centuries to marauding pirates. After several Saracen attacks, the Spanish viceroy, Don Pedro di Toledo, strengthened the defences and reinforced the castle.

Today the port is regularly assaulted by small pleasure boats, but the local fishermen accept the invasion philosophically and the crew of the colourful *paranze* sit on the quay mending their nets and cutting open delicate sea urchins to feed to the passers-by. From the port steep steps lead up to a new restaurant with an idyllic terrace enjoying cool sea breezes and an incomparable view.

La Grotta del Conte
Via Duca del Mare, Castro
Tel. (0836) 92648

In this setting it would be perverse not to eat fish, the house speciality. Pasta is usually prepared with scampi, *datteri* (sea dates) or mussels (*cozze*). For the main course, there is scampi, small lobsters and various local fish depending on the daily catch. These are cooked very simply so that the fine natural flavour can be savoured. A light salad and fresh fruit complete a relaxed meal.

There is a fair selection of regional wines and the newly introduced local Chardonnays and Sauvignons are pleasantly dry and refreshing with the local food.

Price: Inexpensive to moderate: credit cards not accepted
Closed: Wednesday
Location: Above the port

Tricase

*T*ricase was once a small fishing village with a few patrician villas set in the hills, a well-preserved fifteenth century castle and a fine old church. Inevitably it has grown but still remains an attractive small port.

Ristorante Bellavista
Via Borgo Pescatori, Tricase Porto
Tel. (0833) 775097

Elisabetta and Cosimo Musio's restaurant has an enviable position high on the hill with a beautiful view (*bella vista*) of the coast.

Cosima was born in Tricase: but he left to do his military service and later, since there was no work at home, he went to Switzerland. He started to work in hotels and soon realised that he could take his catering experience back to Tricase. By 1981 he was able to build *BellaVista* on land that his father owned. Local fishermen deliver a good supply of fresh fish.

Most visitors tend to order a pasta dish such as *linguine alle cozze* (with mussels). However, there are some very good vegetable dishes like Cosimo's grandmother's recipe for *orecchiette* made with *melanzane* (aubergine/eggplant) and sweet peppers. Although there is always at least one meat dish this is primarily a fish restaurant, offering choices of grilled or baked fish or a light, crisp *fritto misto*. The meal is usually finished with an icecream or a great bowl of fresh fruit, topped with refreshing slices of cool, pink watermelon. Many regional wines are available, including the strong 'Five Roses' or the reliable white Locorotondo.

Price: Inexpensive; credit cards not accepted
Closed: Wednesday; November
Location: overlooking the port.

Bari

*B*ari, today the capital of Puglia, is an intriguing mixture of old and new. The city was constantly invaded from the sea, and Byzantines, Normans, Saracens, French and Spanish have all left their mark. In the old city the street names are self-explanatory. Via Crociata was traversed by the Crusaders about to embark for the Holy Land. Throughout the ages trade has been very important and the Piazza Mercantile, once the business centre with its *colonna infame* (a stone pillar where debtors were whipped), still houses a lively market.

Today Bari's busy modern port sees hundreds of tourists take car ferries to Greece and Yugoslavia every year.

Ai Due Ghiottoni

Via Putignani II, Bari
Tel. (080) 232240

This restaurant is ideally sited in the elegant centre constructed after Napoleon's victory in the early nineteenth century, with its opulent shops in Via Sparano, the luxurious Mincuzzi emporium and Corso Cavour with its great opera house. The restaurant is always very busy, lunch and dinner, so it is essential to book a table.

The name means 'the two gluttons', and every diner becomes a glutton when faced with the cornucopia of regional produce. At the entrance there is a still-life of fresh vegetables, fruit and shellfish, set off by the clear simple decor. There is a printed menu but the team of efficient waiters prefers to bring you a dazzling assortment of their specialities. As well as a selection of traditional vegetable antipasti, fresh mozzarella and richer *burrata* cheeses are on offer, both of them so good in Puglia. This is often followed by *bruschetta con rucola*, garlic toast topped with the sharp, pungent rocket (arugula), an essential flavour in Pugliese cooking. For the first course it is possible to try *fave e cicoria* (beans and bitter salad) or *orecchiette con cime di rape* (pasta ears with turnip tops), served here with the addition of anchovy. Short pasta tubes *sedanini* are served with raw tomatoes and lots of ricotta cheese, very simple but very good, as is the local dish of pasta and white beans, *minestra di cavatelli e fagioli*. Risotto is not a traditional Bari dish, but here I remember an outstanding risotto made with tiny shrimps and squid; an alternative with spinach is equally good.

For the main course most diners choose fish, either a mixed grill, a *fritto misto* or a large fish baked in the oven, depending on the day's catch. A mixture of fish in the *zuppa di pesce* (fish soup) is a great treat. Game is served in season, as are truffles, each truffle accompanied by its certificate of authenticity.

Among the extravagant desserts that appeal to the sweet-toothed, I prefer the simple ricotta tart or a good selection of seasonal exotic fruit. The wine list ranges over a very good choice of regional wines and a few good national wines.

Price: Moderate; Amex, Diners, Visa
Closed: Sunday; August
Location: Central Bari

Taberna Medievale
Via Ospedale di Venere 8, Carbonara di Bari
Tel. (080) 350557

Maria and Filippo Carella's welcoming trattoria, sited in an old olive press near the main square of this suburb of Bari, should not be missed by anyone interested in the traditional cooking of Puglia. The chef, Pietro Abbaticchio, specialises in regional food and the local food historian, Luigi Sada, has researched almost-forgotten recipes which are served here in the *Taberna* and recounted in a fascinating series of booklets published privately by the Carellas for their friends and customers.

Long tables are set out in two rustic-style dining-rooms and there is a tempting display of vegetable antipasti, including sun-dried tomatoes and strange onions called *lampasciuni*, which I think must be an acquired taste. Carbonara is famous for its good bread and the *bruschetta* (savoury toast) here is very tasty. The local pasta curls, called *cavatieddi*, are served with fresh tomato, rocket or arugula and the pungent *ricotta marzolina* cheese. You can order *orecchiette* with a broccoli and cauliflower sauce or a very good stuffed pasta, *agnolotti* filled with ricotta and pistachios. This is a very good place to try the local speciality, *fave e cicoria*. I found it especially good so I asked the chef for his recipe.

This region produces very good lamb, and the *Taberna* serves succulent meat cooked to a turn on the open wood fire, including offal for the more adventurous to try the famous *gnemeriedde*. The traditional *tocchetti di vitello* and the *bracioline* stuffed, rolled veal slices are also carefully prepared and very enjoyable.

Traditional desserts include *pastiera di ricotta* and more creamy concoctions.

There is a fair choice of regional wines, but the house wine is good as you would imagine from a menu which quotes the following: "*Acqua fa male e il vino fa cantare*" (Water is bad for you and wine makes you sing).

Modern marketing usually involves wholesalers, but Filippo Carella buys all the rocket here called *rucola* used in the *Taberna* from an old countryman who gathers the wild leaves in the countryside and then makes his morning rounds on his bike calling out his wares in a plaintive song.

Price: Inexpensive; all major credit cards
Closed: Monday; August
Location: 7 km from central Bari

Monopoli

Monopoli was established in the early Middle Ages and the areas round the port and cathedral have retained their old charm, although further out factories and modern blocks of flats have sprung up. Monopoli, however, makes an ideal base from which to explore one of the most fascinating areas of Italy. The excavations of ancient Egnazia mentioned by the Roman poet, Horace, are only 10 kilometres away on the old Trajan way (via Traiano). Snorkelling in the clear waters just a few metres from the shore you can find large fragments of old amphoras. My very favourite place is the Abbazia Santo Stephanos, a Benedictine Abbey, directly on the sea, flanked by two deep bays with incredibly clear blue water. It is possible to swim across the bays to get a closer look at the eleventh century building and even in the middle of August you can swim peacefully from steps cut in the rocks, avoiding the crowded sandy beach nearby.

Inland, brilliant white Ostuni is nearby, perched high on a hill with its maze of narrow medieval alleys and stone steps, and many small trattorias. Around Monopoli the countryside is studded with *masserie fortificate*, fascinating agricultural settlements that grew up in the sixteenth century.

Il Melograno
Masseria Toricella, Monopoli
Tel. (080) 808656

Camillo Guerra, a Bari antique dealer who loves the Pugliese countryside, decided to restore this sixteenth century *masseria* and to give others a chance to enjoy its particular pleasures. In 1987 he opened a small hotel, *Il Melograno* (The Pomegranate), to provide an unusual setting for business lunches and dinners. The local people soon discovered its elegant dining-room with graceful antiques and the white flowery terraces which are frequently used for weddings and other private parties. Since this is not a restaurant so much as a private centre, it is essential to telephone ahead to book a table. The real beauty of *Il Melograno* is revealed to overnight visitors who can laze by the swimming pool and stroll through the walled garden of citrus trees to reach the private wing which houses a few bedrooms with private patios and modern bathrooms with jacuzzis. The resident chef is equally happy preparing local specialities or international favourites so you can chat to him and plan your meal in advance just as if you were at home.

Price: Moderate; all major credit cards
Closed: a few weeks in winter
Location: 40 km from Bari, direction Fasano

Polignano a Mare

Polignano a Mare, a small town founded by the Greeks and used as a granary by the Roman soldiers marching towards Brindisi, was built where the high, rocky coastline forms a natural stronghold, protecting the inhabitants from surprise sea attacks. Outside the town there are many attractive inlets or *calle*, like the Calle Torre Incina with its sixteenth century defence tower now restored and used as a private house. This *calle* is used by the local fishermen and in the early evening the small coloured boats are moored while the men busily boil tar and repair their nets. Saracen invaders used to pounce on these bays, so until the eighteenth century Polignano had only one road entrance and this gateway was equipped with drawbridge, portcullis and holes through which citizens poured boiling oil on attackers. Today, the same gateway leads to the modern Piazza Garibaldi where Mario Campanella, *Super Mago del Gelo*, the wizard of icecream, sells a variety of good *granitas*, sorbets and fruit icecream.

Ristorante Grotta Palazzese

Via Narciso, Polignano a Mare
Tel. (080) 740261

The modest entrance to this restaurant is inside the old town in one of the old narrow roads lined with white-washed houses. In the summer the people of Polignano leave their doors open to get some breeze and the street becomes a general 'living' area. Since the eighteenth century, the privately-owned grotto has been used for banquets and amorous revels. The present restaurant, which is quite spectacular, is reached by an inside stone staircase. As you go down and down, the smell of the sea becomes stronger, but nothing prepares you for the final sight: a large, solid platform bridges the two sides of the grotto. On one side the tables face the grotto's entrance to the sea and enjoy the constant play of light reflected in the water. On the other side, the tables look down to the clear sea inside and the water makes a perpetual murmur washing against the rocks.

In such a setting the actual food can seem to be of secondary importance, but the local specialities are well-prepared. I have eaten very good pasta with shellfish and the traditional *tiella* and *fave e cicoria* are usually available. There is a very good choice of fresh fish and the lobster are small and full of flavour. There are two or three rich desserts and generous bowls of fruit. The local wine is very pleasant.

The *Grotta Palazzese* is also a hotel and there are several inexpensive rooms with incredible views.

Price: Moderate; Amex, Diners, Visa
Closed: Open all year
Location: Inside the old town walls (leave car outside walls)

Alberobello

*T*hough the traditional rustic huts of Puglia, the *trulli*, are more impressive in the open country of the *Selva di Fasano*, tourists flock to see them in the town of Alberobello, which contains more than 1,000 shimmering white *trulli*.

Il Guercio di Puglia
Largo Martellotta, Alberobello
Tel. (080) 721816

This restaurant is named after the wicked Count of Conversano who was an atrocious overlord in the seventeenth century, earning himself the nickname 'Guercio' because of his squint. The restaurant is set across the wide main road, facing the hurly-burly of central Alberobello and allows you to sit on the terrace enjoying the spectacle. Mima and Giuseppe Buzzerio serve a splendid array of local *antipasti* and for many people at lunch a bottle of the good white Locorotondo would complete the meal, with perhaps a small portion of the local pasta, *orecchiette*. However, there is also good grilled lamb or mixed skewers of meat or tasty local cheese wrapped in bacon.

Price: Inexpensive; all major credit cards
Closed: Wednesday; Christmas and January
Location: central Alberobello, 29 kms from Monopoli

Brindisi

*B*rindisi's good, safe, natural harbour has made it an important port since the seventeenth century, and the Romans ended their Appian Way here with two splendid matching columns. Today one still stands above a wide flight of steps known as the *Scalinata Virgiliana* in honour of the poet, Virgil, who died here on his return from Greece. These steps lead down to the harbour which gained new importance when the Suez Canal opened in the eighteenth century.

Trattoria Le Colonne
Via Colonne 57, Brindisi
Tel. (0831) 28059

This simple trattoria is ideally situated just above the harbour near the Roman columns, and in warm weather you can eat in a peaceful leafy garden, surrounded by olive and fig trees. The cooking is based on good local ingredients, so there is always a choice of vegetable dishes, using artichokes in many guises, broad (fave) beans, *cardi* (edible thistles) depending on the season. The fish is very good here and I enjoyed a tasty pasta dish made with freshly-caught anchovies – *spaghetti con le alici*. The choice is small but the food is carefully prepared from very fresh ingredients. There is usually a home-made dessert, icecream or the good local fruit. There is a small selection of regional wines, including the local Malvasia.

Price: Inexpensive; Amex, Diners, Visa
Closed: Tuesday
Location: above the harbour

~ RECIPE ~
Fave e Cicoria
Broad Beans & Sorrel from the Taberna Medievale

300 grms/10 oz dried or fresh broad beans without skin
400 gms/14 oz cicoria/spinach or sorrel
1 carrot, 1 onion, 1 stick celery, 1 medium sized potato
Salt   3 dl very good quality olive oil, for serving

Cook the dried beans (*fave*) for 3 hours. Drain and cook in 2 litres of lightly-salted water, together with the chopped onion, celery, carrot and potato. After about 25 minutes drain and puree. Cook the *cicoria* in boiling salted water taking care not to overcook and spoil the dark green colour. Drain the *cicoria* and arrange on individual plates with the pureed beans heaped in the middle. Pour a little unheated olive oil and serve hot. Serves 4.

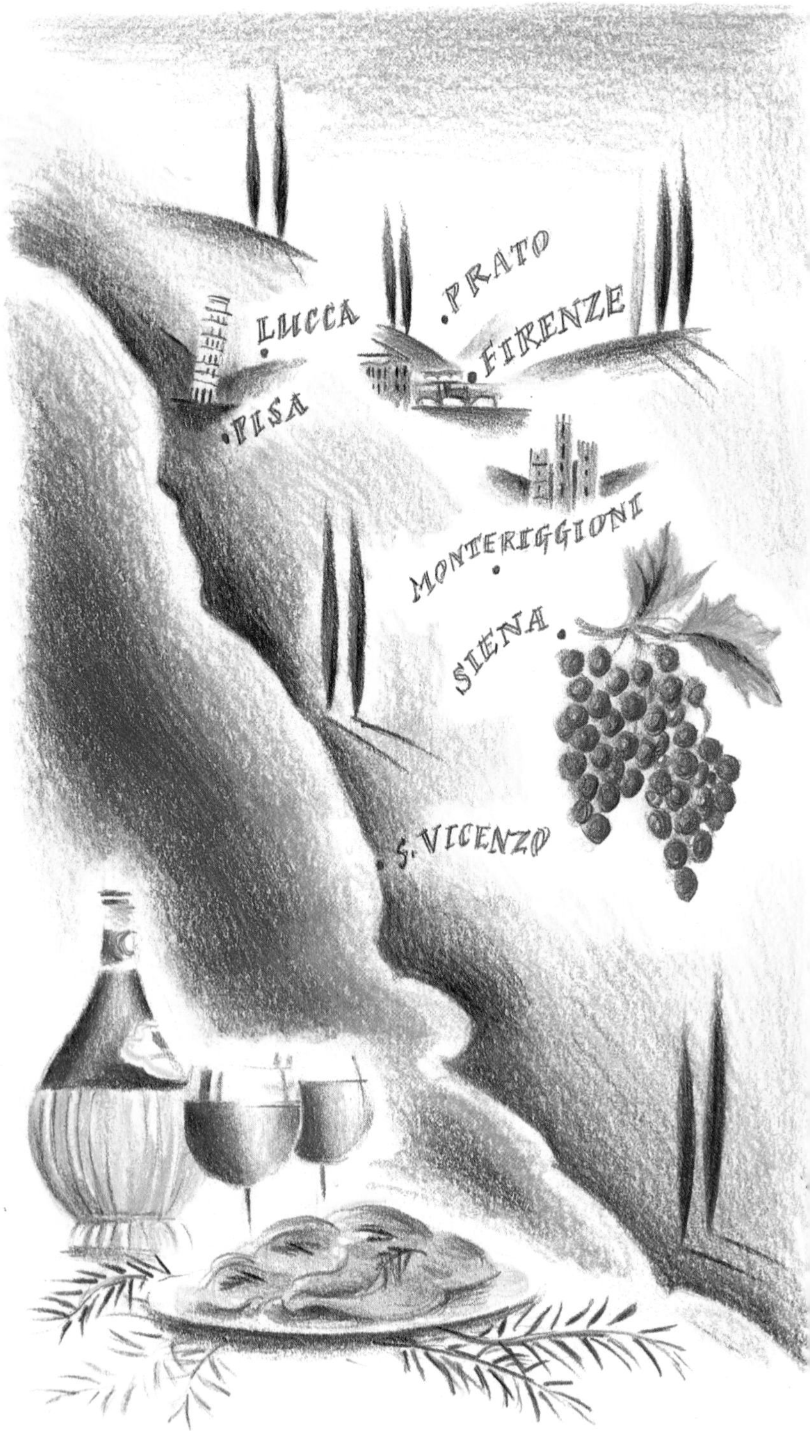
PRATO
LUCCA
FIRENZE
PISA
MONTERIGGIONI
SIENA
S. VICENZO

FLORENCE
& Tuscany

*T*he city of Florence is the jewel of the early Italian Renaissance and is, if anything, today too much appreciated. The Florentines are invaded each year by over a million visitors and their beautifully proportioned squares, austere architecture, finely hung picture galleries and frescoed churches are overrun with admirers.

Similarly, Florentine restaurants are also under pressure, but a fine sense of quality ensures that many good and some great restaurants continue to flourish. Within walking distance of many of the monuments that visitors have come to study, there are friendly and unpretentious trattorias, bars, grand institutions and new experimental gastronomic centres of pilgrimage.

Those merely seeking to sample a wide range of icecreams and sorbets, can call into '*Viroli*' in Via Isola delle Stinche, between Piazza Santa Croce and Piazza San Firenze. This Florentine institution has been run by the same family for three generations, and offers icecreams at simple tables or to take away. '*Gilli*', a small bar and tea room in Piaza della Repubblica, was founded in 1733, and was known to early travellers on the Grand Tour. Today it provides tables where tea or cocktails can be enjoyed in the open air.

Whether the visitor is seeking history, art or architecture, Tuscan gastronomy – or a mixture of all these – some of the very best finds are in the smaller cities of Tuscany, such as Lucca, Siena and Pisa, and the country towns and villages where the best that Tuscany has to offer can be appreciated in peace and tranquillity.

A Tuscan meal starts typically with slices of *finocchiona*, a large *salame* flavoured with fennel seeds, and little *crostini* (toasted bread topped with savoury mixtures of game, offal and mushrooms). Tuscan bread is made without salt and goes very well with the rather salty local ham. Winters are hard in this hilly region and there are many robust soups from the *cucina povera* or home cooking tradition, designed to be nourishing and warming. *Pappa al pomodoro* is one soup that exists in many forms, using ripe tomatoes, bread, olive oil and garlic to make a tasty, filling dish. *Zuppa di fagioli* (bean soup) is made with beans, black cabbage and tomatoes and flavoured with onions, carrots, celery, thyme and rosemary. Slices of garlic toast are placed in the soup bowl and covered with the soup, then the surface is dusted with grated parmesan cheese. Any left-over soup is used the next day to prepare *ribollita* (literally reboiled): the bean soup is covered with finely-sliced onions and a film of olive oil before being put in a hot oven to brown.

White beans were introduced into Tuscan cooking by Alessandro de Medici in the 16th century and they are now an essential ingredient in many dishes. They are used with pasta to make a dense broth to be served as a first course and they are cooked with tomato and sage *all'uccelletto* to make as an accompaniment for meat. Often they are cooked in a narrow-necked, sealed bottle, (*in fiasco*) in order to preserve their flavour and then dressed with olive oil and seasoning.

The most typical Tuscan pasta dishes are *pappardelle alla lepre*, which is very wide ribbon pasta served with hare sauce, and home-made *pici*, a flour and water pasta rolled into thick strings, served with a rich meat sauce. Fresh vegetables are used to make light risotto and there is a heavier version made with meat and chicken livers.

Tuscan meat is very good in quality. The beef for the well-known regional dish, *bistecca alla fiorentina* is obtained from a special breed of *chianana* cattle originally raised by the ancient Romans and Etruscans and used for sacrifices to the pagan gods. The cattle grow very quickly so that even meat from young animals (*vitellone* or big veal) is red, with the added advantage of having very little fat. The *costata* or rib steak, grilled on an open wood fire and seasoned with salt, pepper and olive oil, has a delicious flavour. Another Tuscan speciality is *arosta di maiale*, a lean loin of pork, spiked with cloves and sprigs of rosemary before being roasted. Free-range chickens are cooked in a variety of ways and in winter there are pheasants, partridges and wild boar (*cinghiale*) from the Maremma – the desolate wooded area which lies behind the coast where the cowboys herd their cattle.

The Tuscan coast has its own specialities. Near Livorno they make a delicious fish stew (*cacciucco*) using a large variety of fish and shellfish; and the *triglie rosse di scoglio alla Livornese*, uses the red mullet found lurking near the rocks.

Castagnaccio, a cake made with chestnut flour, pine nuts and herbs used to provide a cheap, easily-carried snack for the carters and foresters working away from home. Those who could not afford the olive oil needed in the recipe made *pattona*, equally filling, with chestnut flour and water. Nowadays, chestnut flour has become very expensive and *castagnaccio* is reserved as a treat, although it is rather too plain for many tastes.

The town of Prato, near Florence, produces hard, nutty biscuits (cookies) *cantucci* which are served with sweet wine (*vino santo*). Siena provides richer sweets, such as *ricciarelli* –

diamond-shaped marzipan lozenges – believed to have been brought back to Siena from the Crusades. The origins of the famous Sienese *panforte* made from almonds, hazelnuts, candied fruit and spices has caused much learned discussion: in 'The Inferno', Dante talks of a certain Niccolo who discovered a cake made with cloves, and historians have traced this reference to Siena's Niccolo Salinbeni who made many voyages to the Orient and found a bread made with honey, cloves and other spices.

The famous local wine, Chianti, is ideally suited to traditional Tuscan cooking, and the *gallo nero* (black cockerel), the Denominazione di Origine Controllata mark designed for wine produced in the Chianti area, used to dominate the scene. Recently, however, many restaurants have made their cooking lighter to suit modern tastes and

new white wines, like the marvellous Vergena or Light
Antinori Poggio alle Gazze, have been developed to go with
this more delicate food. In some towns it is even quite hard
today to find the traditional *bistecca alla fiorentina* since there
has been an increased interest in the new food and wine. An
old Tuscan proverb says, '*Il pan di casa stufa*' – 'the bread at
home gets boring' – and everyone now is busy trying new
ideas for bread and everything else.

Il Latini
Via dei Palchetti 6, Florence
Tel. (055) 210916

You do not go to *Il Latini* for a romantic meal *à deux*, nor to discuss confidential business deals. Traditional Tuscan food is served here at long communal tables where you plunge into conversation with people from widely different backgrounds. On a recent visit for a solitary, rather late lunch my table emptied before I had finished eating and Giovanni immediately whisked me to another lively table where I was welcomed with great warmth by an animated group of assorted customers. The Latini family aim to nourish the spirit as well as the body (they even have an annual literary prize) and what is good food without good company?

The trattoria started life as a humble wine shop, or *fiaschetteria*, at the end of the last century, but when Angiola Latini handed over to his nephew, Narciso, in 1950, Narciso began to serve bread rolls stuffed full of prosciutto and *salame* from his native Certaldo. He also served some hot soups, prepared at home by his wife, Maria. Local workmen came regularly for their mid-morning break and whole generations of students survived because of Maria's generous portions and Narciso's equally generous '*Pagherai domani*' (you can pay tomorrow) – which extended indefinite credit to those in need since which *domani* was never specified. A loyal clientele gradually developed and in 1964 the *fiashetteria* moved to fresh premises in Via Palchetti, in the stables of the Rucellai palace. Even then space was limited, so Maria still had to cook the food at home and carry it to the trattoria. Two years later, when the Arno flooded, the trattoria was destroyed, but the Latini family moved into the mud-filled streets serving food and drink to the armies of rescue workers.

When the trattoria was restored it was enlarged to provide an adequate kitchen area and three dining-rooms with space to seat up to 200 people. The tradition of good home-cooking has been kept alive, and today the sons, Giovanni and Torello, give the same warm welcome and value for money. Prices are kept within the ordinary workers' reach and only half the places can be reserved in advance, the other half being freely available to anyone who drops in. Each table carries two large flasks of chianti which are circulated freely and replenished when necessary, with nobody keeping count of how much any one person drinks.

It is possible to start with *finocchiona*, *salsiccia di cinghiale* (a dry sausage of wild boar), *prosciutto*, or fresh cheeses like ricotta or *raveggiuolo*. The traditional nourishing soups, *ribollita*, *pappa al pomodoro* and *fagioli con farro* (bean soup), are always on the menu.

Here you also find all the traditional Tuscan main courses – meat stewed in good red wine and various grilled meats (the quality of the meat is superb) – served with tender white beans and all the vegetables that are in season. *Il Latini* also serves a light crisp mixture of vegetables fried in batter.

Although there is a good choice of desserts and fresh fruit, most people finish their meal with *cantuccini con vino santo* (hard, nutty biscuits to be dunked in little glasses of sweet wine), a speciality from nearby Prato.

Price: Very inexpensive, credit cards not accepted
Closed: Monday & Tuesday lunch; July 20-August 8, Christmas
Location: Central Florence, off Via Vigna Nuova

Ristorante Sabatini
Via Panzani 41/43, Florence
Tel. (055) 282802

Sabatini is an elegant old restaurant with a long history of service to the rich and famous. When the Sabatini family decided to give up the restaurant it was taken over by a team of five successful restaurateurs, each with his own field of professional expertise. This team has succeeded in keeping standards consistently high, and today *Sabatini* is the Florentine restaurant for all seasons and all customers. The premises are spacious and comfortable, the service is exemplary and the comprehensive menu satisfies all requirements.

The long list of first courses is made up of Tuscan soups and pasta dishes from all regions of Italy. The main course offerings follow the same pattern with 10 daily suggestions for meat dishes plus a selection of grilled meats and fresh fish. The dessert trolley is full of sweet temptations like *tiramisu*, (the Venetian speciality made from chocolate, cream cheese and liqueur).

The wine list demands serious study, and here again the choice is overwhelming.

Price: Expensive; Amex, Diners, Visa
Closed: Monday; July 1-15
Location: Central Florence, near the station

Cibreo
Via dei Macci 118, Florence
Tel. (050) 2341100

Cibreo is a very unusual Italian restaurant in that it does not serve pasta. When I first overheard the charming Fabio Picchi explaining this to a puzzled foreign visitor I thought there must be some profound culinary philosophy behind this outrageous statement since even the most *nouvelle* of Italian chefs do not dare to lay hands on pasta, the sacred heart of any Italian meal. When I asked Fabio why he did not serve pasta he was disarmingly frank. He likes to cook or at least oversee the preparation of every dish personally yet at the same time he likes to play the host in the restaurant. Since it is impossible to be in two places at the same time he has ruthlessly banished pasta which needs to be prepared freshly at the last minute for every customer.

Fabio's wife, Benedetta, is the only person he will delegate to in the kitchen, but since they have four children her professional time is strictly limited. The Picchi have known each other since they were 14 years old, when Fabio wooed her with little gastronomic presents, beginning with a lovingly prepared butter and anchovy sandwich. They started *Cibreo* together nine years ago, learning as they went along. The restaurant has enjoyed great success, and recently was expanded a little. Benedetta and Fabio have also opened a small speciality food and wine shop.

The restaurant is very welcoming, and in warm weather it is

possible to sit outside under the cream umbrellas in the little piazza near Sant'Ambrogio market which provides many of the fresh vegetables that appear on the menu. As soon as you are seated you are offered a glass of white wine, and your glass is replenished while you sample a variety of interesting 'nibbles', including an unusual mousse made from ricotta cheese. Everything is beautifully presented down to the tiny bread roll, made just the right size to nestle in the bowl of your spoon. Fabio comes to each table to explain the dishes he has prepared – there is no written menu – and to suggest appropriate wines. On his recommendation I discovered an excellent 'Bruno di Rocca' produced in Greve, in Chianti, by Vecchie Terre di Montefili.

Passato di peperoni is a very beautiful pale yellow first course, a little like a soup, made from pureed sweet peppers. The flavour is delicate and it is difficult to choose between this and *Cibreo's* very individual version of the traditional *pappa al pomodoro*. Here the tomato dish is served tepid and the consistency is so thick it can be eaten with a fork – a fragrant creation made with lots of fresh basil and red tomatoes cooked very quickly so that all the colour and flavour are preserved. If this is on the menu, do try it. Another delightful first course is inspired by the extravagant Neapolitan pasta dish *bucatini alla flamande*. Little individual moulds are lined with green beans and filled with a light tuna fish mousse. When turned out, the green beans give the same effect as the more usual bucatini pasta. A very decorative and interesting combination of tastes and textures.

The main courses of fish and meat are equally imaginative and varied. I have very fond memories of small sole fillets rolled up and served with a fine green onion sauce, and tender leg of lamb rolled, stuffed and cooked to perfection. One of the most simple yet masterly dishes is made from the caps of *funghi porcini*, seasoned and then cooked in foil. When the foil is opened the aroma is heady.

Among the rich selection of desserts I have particularly enjoyed a very crisp, light lemon tart, and a vanilla bavarian cream served with fresh raspbery sauce.

Cibreo is the ideal place to try light new dishes inspired by traditional Italian cooking. The many small portions are stimulating but not too heavy.

Price: Moderate to expensive; Amex, Diners, Visa
Closed: Sunday, Monday; January 1-7; April 4-10; July 26-Sept 9
Location: Central Florence, near Sant'Ambrogio market

La Capannina di Sante

Piazza Ravenna (Corner Ponte da Verrazzano), Florence
Tel. (055) 688345

Sante Collesano is an experienced fisherman from Sicily with an instinctive flair for cooking fish and an innate sense of hospitality. These qualities have inevitably led him to his *capannina* on the banks of the Arno. It needs some poetic licence to call this elegantly pretty restaurant a 'straw hut' but the terrace does have a straw roof and the setting right on the river bank is peaceful and rustic.

Sante himself drives to the coast early each morning to select his fish, and he bases his daily menu on what is available – sometimes fish from Italian waters, sometimes flown in from France or more exotic coasts, but the quality is always superb.

There is a good list of Italian and French wines. On my last visit I chose a Sauvignon from Friuli which went very well with the series of little antipasti Sante brings to whet the appetite while the first course is being cooked to order. The menu changes daily but there are usually some tasty soups made with mussels or other molluscs such as sea dates (*datteri*). A glistening black risotto made with little squid and their ink is in dramatic contrast to a delicate white dish of *spaghetti alla Posillipo*, made with large clams (*vongole veraci*), where flecks of parsley provide the only touch of colour. However, the house speciality is the most mouth-watering of all – *spaghetti alla Sante*, made with *datteri*, mussels, prawns, clams and *seppie* (cuttlefish), cooked briefly with white wine, garlic, parsley and a touch of tomato.

For the main course there is a mixed grill of fish, scampi and prawns or lobster, or a prized fish like *branzino* (sea bass) cooked simply in the oven.

During the late summer evenings when the normal menu is no longer available, since the staff have gone home, Sante prepares a Spanish *paella alla Valenciana* for his special guests who can enjoy a whiff of Spain on the banks of the Arno.

Price: Moderate; Visa
Closed: Sunday, Monday lunch; part of August; Christmas
Location: On the river Arno, at Ponte da Verrazzano

Enoteca Pinchiorri
Via Ghibellina 87, Florence
Tel. (055) 242757

The name *Enoteca Pinchiorri* has become synonymous with exquisite wine and fine food. Giorgio Pinchiorri has an incredible collection of wines, and his wife, Annie Feoldé, daughter of a Nice hotelier, who started out providing little delicacies to serve along with his wine, has become a brilliant chef. Annie has no formal catering training, but when she came to Florence to polish up her Italian, she turned to restaurant work in order to survive. She met Giorgio, and this meeting not only changed the course of her life, it also transformed the Florentine restaurant scene.

Enoteca Pinchiorri is in the Santa Croce area, housed in a beautiful fifteenth century building, with a small garden and courtyard where meals can be eaten in the warmer months. The setting is very elegant and the tables are beautifully furnished. Annie has a young team of helpers who provide impeccable service. She recruits from families already employed to create a feeling of harmony and team spirit.

The cooking is new and exciting and it is impossible to predict which dishes will be offered. The food is still chosen to enhance the wines, and each diner usually samples four or five superb wines in an evening. There are three menus which change according to season: one menu is based exclusively on fish; another, *la cucina toscana ritrovata*, is developed from old traditional recipes which Annie has researched and adapted to make them lighter and more acceptable to modern tastes; and finally there is a glorious *cucina creativa*, for which Annie draws endless unusual combinations from the daily market produce. (It is possible to order *à la carte* but the restaurant expects customers to order a full meal.) I have always ordered *la cucina creativa* and sat back to enjoy a series of delectable surprises, each accompanied by a different wine, each dish a memorable discovery.

Price: *Very expensive (special lunch at a third of normal price); Amex*
Closed: *Sunday, Monday lunch; Christmas and August*
Location: *Central Florence, near Santa Croce*

Ristorante Dino

Via Ghibellina 51, Florence
Tel. (055) 241452

Dino Casini, a Florentine with a passion for good Tuscan food and wine, opened his first little trattoria in 1960 with such success that in 1966 he moved to this larger, more elegant restaurant which consists of three vaulted rooms in an old fourteenth century building near the house of Michelangelo. Dino is an expert sommelier and all his wines are listed at a very fair price with less than the usual mark-up.

This restaurant is very much a family affair. Dino and his wife, Renza, create the menu and while Renza is busy in the kitchen with her small band of helpers, their son, Massimo, and daughter, Sonia, give smiling helpful service in the restaurant.

The menu is based on traditional Tuscan cooking and all the regional specialities are here – tasty *crostini*, robust *ribollita*, succulent *bistecca alla fiorentina*, and tender white beans (*fagioli bianchi*) glistening in their dressing of extra-virgin olive oil. Dino and Renza have also perfected a lighter range of old and new dishes using fresh vegetables and wild herbs from the surrounding hills. The *risotto della Renza* is fragrant with herbs, and *spaghetti alla Dino*, flavoured with celery, carrots and sweet peppers.

From his researches into elaborate recipes from Florentine history, Dino has devised *stracotto del Granduca*, based on a dish served at banquets in the time of the Medicis. A large piece of superb Tuscan beef is spiked with garlic, rosemary ,almonds, pine nuts, mint and cinnamon and then cooked very slowly in good chianti wine. The finished dish exudes a tantalising mixture of aromas. The *garetto Ghibellino*, taken from another old recipe, cooks shin of pork with sage and celery.

To finish, there are various icecreams and some delicious Tuscan desserts which Renza makes with great expertise.

Price: *Moderate; Amex, Diners, Visa*
Closed: *Sunday evening, Monday; July 30 to August 27*
Location: *Central Florence, near the house of Michelangelo*

Osteria Numero Uno
Via del Moro 22, Florence
Tel. (055) 284897

Osteria Numero Uno is in the heart of old Florence, just round the corner from Borgo Ognissanti where it started life at Number One, hence its name. Gianni Girardi, originally from Verona, fell in love with Florence when he came to do his military service in 1958 and resolved to do any job available to stay there. After working as a trainee waiter at the famous Sabatini restaurant, he opened his first 'Numero Uno' employing the venerable chef, Masino, who had previously worked for some of the great families in Florence. When Masino retired, Aldo Magnagno, the present chef, came from Venice to collaborate as Gianni's partner.

In this austere old building with its vaulted ceiling and massive fireplace the menu changes frequently according to the season. The pasta is all *fatte in casa* (home-made), and the *sfogliatine di ricotta e basilico* (envelopes of ricotta cheese and basil) melt in the mouth. Aldo's Venetian heritage is seen in wonderful rice dishes, including *risotto agli asparagi* in the asparagus season and *risotto al peperone dolce* (with sweet peppers). The delicate *carpaccio di salmone* delights the palate, and *tagliata di Lorenzo de Medici* is a must for anyone craving good rare roast beef. There is always a well-furnished dessert trolley with light modern inventions and rich, substantial sweets like *torta della nonna*.

There is as good selection of Tuscan wines or you can settle for the pleasant housewine, 'La Sala', from San Casciano. It appears in a large flask but, in good Tuscan tradition, you only pay for what you drink.

Price: *Moderate; Visa*
Closed: *Sunday; August*
Location: *Central Florence, near Piazza Ognissanti*

Coco Lezzone
Via del Parioncino 26, Florence
Tel. (055) 287178

Coco Lezzone is an old Florentine eating-house two steps from the elegant Via Tornabuoni. The name literally means 'the dirty cook', but don't recoil in disgust – this is just a humorous allusion to the Italian tendency to distrust any cook wearing a pristine apron. A man who dirties his apron can be trusted to produce serious, down-to-earth food.

The two dining-rooms follow the same utilitarian, no-nonsense theme. It is not possible to reserve a table, so be sure to come early if you want to avoid waiting for a place. The food is good and the fair price attracts hungry hordes.

Regional specialities are well-prepared by the cook-owner Piero Paoli – despite his clean apron – and his brother and co-owner, Franco, keeps delays to the minimum at the long tables. They provide a feast of Tuscan food: *pasta e fagioli* (pasta and beans), *ribollita*, *pappa al pomodoro*, and the more difficult to find *minestrone di lampredotto* (substantial vegetable soup). The grilled meat is excellent.

Price: Inexpensive; credit cards not accepted
Closed: Sunday, Tuesday evening in winter: Saturday, Sunday in summer
Location: Central Florence, off Via Tornabuoni

Leo in Santa Croce
Via Torta 7, Florence
Tel. (055) 210829

Leo in Santa Croce is a comfortable, family-run trattoria right in the heart of medieval Florence. Leo Bosciolini, the owner, was born in Perugia, an area famous for its good cooking.

The menu is rich and varied with many regional specialities. yet Leo's Perugian heritage is seen in the liberal use of black truffles, and the inexpensive house wine is an Umbrian red. The pasta dishes range from the delicate *tagliolini al tartufo* (with truffles) to the robust *pappardelle alla lepre* (pasta with hare sauce), and you will find *ravioli di patate* (potato dumplings) and the hearty *zuppa contadina*, which is a very early version of the famous Tuscan *ribollita*. For the main course there is a good selection of meat and fish, carefully chosen by Leo. The menu bears the warning: *La fretta e la nemica della buona cucina* ('Haste is the enemy of good food'); Leo has no patience with restless customers who expect 'fast food'.

Leo's daughter, Paola, takes an active part in running the restaurant and her husband, Fabrizio, a keen young chef, works wonders in the kitchen. Leo prides himself on offering good food at a very fair price and each day he likes to suggest to his clients what items offer best value for money.

Price: Moderate; Amex, Diners, Visa
Closed: Mondays; July 20 to August 20
Location: Central Florence, near Santa Croce church

Villa San Michele

Via di Doccia, Fiesole (Florence)
Tel. (055) 59451

Villa San Michele must have the most beautiful view in Florence. The villa used to be an old monastery and Michelangelo himself is said to have designed the facade of the bulding which is set high in the hills in beautiful gardens surrounded by cypress trees. Today the villa is a luxury hotel and from its large flowering terrace you can enjoy a spectacular view looking down on Florence and the Arno. In good weather it is possible to eat on this terrace, and what could be more idyllic than to sit absorbed by the view, with a cool glass of wine and a good plate of pasta. The main menu seems to offer luxury international food, and, inevitably, hotel food has certain limitations. However, the service is charming and it is a rare pleasure to eat in such beautiful surroundings. English tea, served in the afternoon, is a relaxing treat.

Price: Very expensive; all major credit cards
Closed: November to March
Location: 8 km from centre of Florence on the road to Fiesole

La Vecchia Cucina
Viale de Amicis 1, Florence
Tel. (055) 660143

This is one of my favourite restaurants in Florence, a short taxi ride away from the centre on the way up to Fiesole. On a long journey it can also make a memorable stopping point because it is just 2 kilometres from the *autostrada* exit, Firenze Sud.

Although '*la vecchia cucina*' means old-style cooking, Alessandro Franceschetti's menu is carefully balanced between old and new. He changes his menu each week to make full use of seasonal produce and there is usually a choice of five or six items for each course. There is a good wine list, and in summer I have enjoyed the light white Antinori Poggio alle Gazze.

The Franceschettis originate from Emilia Romagna where egg-enriched pasta was first invented, and Alessandro's mother personally makes the wonderful fresh pasta for the restaurant. I have particulary relished her delicate *cappelletti* stuffed with a mixture of *melanzane* (aubergines/egg-plant) and cheese, and ravioli with tuna fish and capers. In the summer heat, my wilting appetite was jolted to life when confronted with a plate of pasta flavoured with fresh uncooked tomatoes, and fresh basil.

Fresh vegetables play an important part in the menu, and the *fritto misto* of deep-fried *zucchini*, *funghi porcini*, melanzane and marrow (squash) flowers makes an agreeable main course. The meat dishes are well chosen and often combine unusual flavours like tender beef with a black olive paste.

The choice of desserts is irresistible, with my favourite being a raspberry soufflé served with a small glass of *fragolino*, the sweet red wine home-made from *uva fragole* (strawberry-flavoured Italian grapes).

Price: Moderate to expensive; Amex
Closed: July 25-August 25
Location: 2 kilometres from autostrada exit Firenze Sud

Taverna del Bronzino
Via del Ruote 25r, Florence
Tel. (055) 495220

The main dining-room of this well-established Florentine restaurant in a fifteenth century building is an austerely proportioned former studio, where a pupil of the painter Bronzino lived and worked. The elegant simplicity of the building, to which a small garden courtyard has recently been added, is backed up by an enterprising and well-cooked repertoire of classic dishes and a well-stocked wine list.

The restaurant prides itself on serving not only Tuscan food – whose soups and beef stews they feel are at their best in winter – but also lighter, more experimental and international dishes, such as grilled salmon with ginger sauce, and veal with asparagus. Pride of place on the evening menu usually goes to a large piece of good Tuscan beef.

Among the antipasti are stewed fish and artichokes, *crostini*, and strips of smoked goose with salad. The pasta dishes include *tortelloni al cedro* (veal-stuffed pasta with a lime and cream sauce) and *tagliolini al tartufo*, with a grating of fresh truffle. As well as good Florentine steaks, *osso buco*, liver and game are all featured among the main dishes, with spinach, beans, artichokes and asparagus as vegetables.

Patronised in the main at lunchtime by Florentine businessmen and women, the restaurant is only a 15 minute walk from the Duomo and central splendours of the city, yet few tourists make the discovery.

Price: *Moderate to expensive; credit cards not accepted*
Closed: *Sunday; August*
Location: *central Florence, between P. San Marco and P. Independenza*

Da Graziella
Maiano, Fiesole
Tel. (055) 599963

Da Graziella is a delightful rustic trattoria high in the hills above Florence at Maiano, where the road comes to an end by the famous cave. Here in a peaceful rural setting you can eat good food carefully prepared from fresh local produce at an extremely reasonable price.

In the spring of 1988, Ugo and Giovanni Salis, two brothers

from Sardinia with some previous restaurant experience in Tuscany behind them, joined Siberiano Capaccioli, cook and sommelier, and his son, Carlo, to take over this old country bar and trattoria. The setting has endless possibilities and already this family venture has taken great strides forward. Their delicious fresh pasta is stuffed with spinach and ricotta cheese supplied daily by their fellow Sards from flocks of sheep in the neighbouring hills. These shepherds also provide the excellent lamb served in the trattoria. Like all the meat here, this is cooked over an open charcoal grill and the air is full of tantalising aromas. Vegetables bought from local market gardeners provide Siberiano with the ingredients for a rich array of antipasto and a hearty *ribollita*.

The house wine is a red or white 'Lorenzo Bulloni', and Siberiano has carefully chosen nine reds, nine whites and a *spumante* for his first wine list, a modest beginning but showing the same promise apparent everywhere in this happy trattoria. The warmth and enthusiasm here make a striking contrast to some of the tourist-weary trattorias. Cool in the height of summer, but warm in winter with a great blazing fire, *Da Graziella* is a treat not to be missed.

Price: *Very inexpensive; credit cards not accepted*
Closed: *Always open*
Location: *8 km from Florence, towards Fiesole*

Prato

Prato, 20 kilometres north-west from Florence is well worth a short visit to admire the fourteenth century castle. The poet Robert Browning, who lived in Florence for many years, visited Prato frequently when he was writing his dramatic monologue, 'Fra Lippo Lippi', to admire the artist's frescoes in the Duomo.

Trattoria Bruno
Via Verdi 12, Prato
Tel. (0574) 23810

This trattoria is situated in a narrow medieval street just behind the castle. The interior is very pleasing with light, modern decor. When the present owner, Osvaldo Baroncelli, took over from his father he kept the traditional menu but introduced some light, modern variations. There is an imaginative series of antipasti consisting of vegetable terrines, delicate fillets of salmon trout and little omelettes made with artichokes, asparagus or sweet peppers. A good choice of home-made pasta dishes offers ravioli stuffed with a potato and pumpkin mixture or ricotta cheese, and other pasta served with sauces made from the fresh vegetables in season . Bruno also offers traditional Tuscan soups, and the *pappa al pomodoro* is tasty and nourishing. The main course offers some interesting dishes like boned lamb stuffed with puréed cabbage and duck breast cooked with *aceto balsamico* (aromatic vinegar) and sweet peppers. The desserts are light and airy, based on fruit in season. The legendary expert, Andrea Trinci, has drawn up a superb list of Italian wines.

Price: Moderate; Amex, Diners and Master Charge
Closed: Thursday evening, Sunday; August
Location: 20 kilometres NW of Florence off A11 Autostrada

Lucca

*L*ucca is a delightful old town 74 kilometres from Florence, heading towards the sea. Its Roman past can be savoured in the Piazza del Anfiteatreo, where the tall, narrow medieval houses have been built on the foundations of the old amphitheatre forming an oval piazza. The Renaissance ramparts are in good condition and it is still possible to stroll along parts of the walls under shady trees admiring

the roofs of the old palaces and churches. Today Lucca is a thriving city, producing superb olive oil which is used to good effect in the local traditional cooking based on vegetables, grain and game.

Buca di Sant'Antonio
Via della Cervia 1, Lucca
Tel. (0583) 055881

Over 150 years ago this used to be an old coaching inn, providing rooms, food and stables for travellers heading to and from Rome. Today, still tucked away in a mews not too far from San Frediano church, it has become a welcoming rustic trattoria serving good local food. There are hearty soups made from dried beans and peas and *farro* (spelt), pasta dishes like *pappardelle alla lepre* (pasta with hare sauce) or *tacconi*, a local square pasta, served with a sauce of rabbit or *funghi porcini*. The main course offers dishes like tasty lamb stewed with olives, stuffed rabbit or pigeons cooked on the spit. For dessert there are various fruit tarts and in winter the traditional *castagnaccio* made with chestnut flour and ricotta cheese.

There is a fair choice of regional wines.

Price: Moderate; Amex, Diners and Visa
Closed: Sunday evening, Monday; the last three weeks in July
Location: Central Lucca, near San Frediano church

La Mora
Via Sesto di Moriano 104, Ponte a Moriano
Tel. (0583) 57109

A trip to Ponte a Moriano north of Lucca to enjoy a meal at *La Mora* is well worth the effort. *La Mora* was originally an old posting house on the road to Garfagnana. It has been run by the same family since 1867 but the years have inevitably seen great changes. When Pellegrino Brunicardi took over just after the war in 1946, La Mora was a simple trattoria serving fried fish from the nearby river Serchio, tasty bread baked in a wood oven and good local wine. Today, *La Mora* is an elegant restaurant with comfortable dining-rooms, and a lovely garden shaded by a pergola. The present owners, Sauro and his wife, Angela, while retaining all the original local specialities (Sauro's mother, Assunta, still makes all the fresh pasta), have introduced several dishes which have evolved naturally from Lucca's culinary traditions. The resulting menu is rich and varied.

Among the antipasti I have enjoyed minute fried fish called *delizie del Serchio*, a chicken and pine nut salad, trout fillets with artichokes, and a sweet red pepper terrine. The pasta is very light, thanks to Signora Assunta, and the ravioli perfumed with marjoram or the pappardelle with duck sauce are irresistible. On a visit one May, I enjoyed a perfect risotto made from young, fresh asparagus.

For main courses you can choose from several fresh-water fish dishes, ranging from the traditional fried Serchio fish to salmon trout in a citrus fruit sauce. Among the many interesting meat dishes, guinea fowl, rabbit and pigeon jostle for place beside lamb, beef and veal. I have warm memories of lamb served with fresh garlic and spinach sauce, guinea fowl cooked with *funghi porcini*, and a stuffed sliced rabbit. The desserts, based mainly on fresh fruit, are light and beautifully presented and they make a fitting end to a memorable meal.

There is a very good wine list and Sauro is happy to suggest a good local wine to enhance your meal. Opposite the restaurant the family have opened an *enoteca* selling good wine and olive oil, where the wines are kept cool by the underground stream which runs beneath the building.

Price: *Moderate; Amex, Diners and Visa*
Closed: *Wednesday evening and Thursday*
Location: *9 kilometres north of Lucca, route to Bagni di Lucca*

Vipore
Pieve Santo Stefano
Tel. (0583) 52945

The hills outside Lucca used to be infested with brigands, but happily nowadays the drive to Pieve Santo Stefano is quite uneventful, although it can be quite difficult to track down *Vipore*, set high in the hills in an eighteenth century country house. From the cool flowery gardens you can enjoy a panoramic view of Lucca and the Tuscan landscape.

In 1964 Rosa and Pietro Casella decided to take over the property and turn it into a restaurant. Rosa had been a cook in many of the great local houses and Pietro worked magic grilling meat on aromatic wood fires. Their son, Cesare, grew up in this restaurant and he has inherited his parents love of good food, transforming simple dishes by a judicious use of herbs from his kitchen garden.

The antipasti consist of traditional *crostini*, two dried meat combinations and a delightful warm salad. For the pasta course there is a choice of local fresh pasta (*tacconi*) served with *funghi porcini* or a rabbit sauce, or a deceptively simple *macceroncini* cooked with fresh tomatoes, pecorino cheese and thyme. There are also some unusual soups like the fennel and lettuce *klinai*, recently re-discovered by Cesare, which takes its name from the Etruscan terracotta dish *triclinio*. Cesare also serves more homely soups like lentil and *farro* – spelt broth. For the main course, among the long list of meat dishes, I recommend beef fillet in a marjoram sauce, or pork cooked with rosemary and shallots. There is a small selection of home-made desserts and good fresh seasonal fruit.

There is a very good wine list chosen by Cesare with a keen eye for value for money. He finds most Lucca red wines overpriced so he prefers not to sell them, listing other good regional reds or an inexpensive young wine produced by a neighbouring farmer. This wine, light peony in colour, is quite pleasant. I also enjoyed a fresh local white wine named after Maria Teresa who became Duchess of Lucca in 1842.

Do remember to reserve a table in advance because Cesare likes to welcome every guest and explain the menu himself. Bruna Ricci has been helping serve at the tables for over 22 years and she is a mine of local information.

Price: Moderate; Amex and Diners
Closed: Monday and Tuesday lunch. Holiday varies from year to year so check
Location: 9 km W. of Lucca, off S439

Pisa

*P*isa, where Galileo taught at the medieval university, preserves at its centre a great series of buildings, including the cathedral and the famous Leaning Tower. Pisa is still an important university town, enlarged each season with many thousands of visitors.

Al Ristoro dei Vecchi Macelli
Via Volturno 49, Pisa
Tel. (050) 20422

This is one of my favourite restaurants in Tuscany. Although it is indeed in front of the old slaughter-house (*macelli*), this is no ancient eating-house serving robust dishes of offal and cheap meat cuts. When the 'Ristoro' was opened in 1981, Stefano Vanni had no family catering tradition behind him. Yet all his family have now brought passion and dedication to this new enterprise and their enthusiasm and expertise have made this a delightfully warm, polished restaurant where the service is always attentive and the food imaginative. Stefano's mother, Miranda, reigns in the kitchen, and his wife, Ida, in addition to following her own independent profession, shares their involvement and spends her spare time in the dining-room helping customers to choose their meal with charming authority.

The restaurant is housed in a fifteenth century building which was originally the site of the Santa Chiara church, and the old crypt lies sealed beneath the kitchens. The beamed ceilings and dark wood floors of the dining-rooms are decorated in an elegantly simple style with large silver lamps illuminating

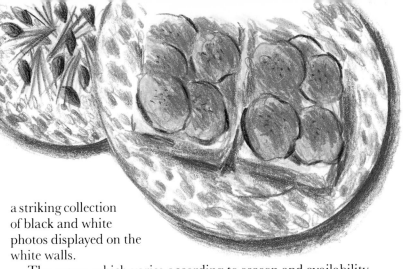

a striking collection
of black and white
photos displayed on the
white walls.

The menu, which varies according to season and availability,
offers suggestions from *terra o mare* (land or sea). Every dish is
beautifully presented. Among the many antipasti, I remember
lightly steamed prawns served in a basil sauce with a little fresh
diced tomato, and a delicate chicken mousse studded with black
truffles from Umbria. The pasta, all made by hand by Miranda
Vanni, is so light it melts in the mouth. I love her little green pasta
bags stuffed with sea bass or scallops and served with shrimps in
a pale orange sauce, as well as the white *tortelli* filled with wild
herbs and served with fresh ripe tomato purée topped by sprigs of
basil and wonderful green olive oil.

The main courses are equally delicious. I remember with
pleasure a fillet of fresh bream (*marmora*) in a pale caramel-
coloured almond sauce. Among the good selection of unusual
meat dishes you can find pigeon, rabbit and wild boar as well as
the more common veal.

Italian desserts are often a little disappointing but here the
sweet-toothed will be in seventh heaven. From a long, enticing list
I particularly liked a cold pear and apple soufflé served with an
avocado sauce.

The Vannis have a very extensive wine list and I first
discovered the marvellous white 'Vergena' when Ida suggested to
me that it would go equally well with all the dishes
I had ordered.

Price: Moderate to expensive; Amex, Diners, Visa
Closed: Sunday, Wednesday; January 1-8, August 3-28
Location: central Pisa, near Ciltadella

Il Nuraghe
Via Mazzini 58, Pisa
Tel. (050) 44368

It would be a mistake to miss Pisa's *Nuraghe* simply because the chef and owner, Augusto Pila, is not a Tuscan. He has absorbed a feeling for Tuscan cooking during his working years spent in Pisa, but he still retains strong links with his native Sardinia, and a number of Sardinian specialities appear on his menu.

Il Nuraghe enjoys a faithful following of regulars. At lunchtime several tables are set with partly-consumed bottles of wine and as the customers arrive they greet each other like the old friends they are.

Tasty antipasti include smoked tuna fish salad, marinated prawns and lobster, and wild boar *salame*. The first course selection offers vegetable dishes like risotto with peas, pasta shells with artichokes. For the main course there is a good choice of meat and fish dishes.

Several Sardinian desserts are usually offered and the wine list is small but well-chosen.

Price: Inexpensive; Amex
Closed: Monday
Location: Between Arno and Piazza Vittorio Emmanuele II

Limonaia
Vicolo dei Ruschi 2/a, Pisa
Tel. Pizzeria 41251 Restaurant 42535

Wriggling off the Via Francesco in Pisa is the tiny alley of Vicolo dei Ruschi, where the tired traveller, whose sense of balance has been given a bad shock by climbing the Leaning Tower, can enter a restful and enchanting garden, the high brick walls covered with roses and jasmine, the paths flanked by lemon trees. At the end of the garden is a sixteenth century building that has been transformed into two modern eating places. A simple but well-designed pizzeria is on the ground floor and upstairs a bar and restaurant.

The menu is equally a combination of traditional Tuscan ingredients and modern innovations. Among the antipasti are stuffed artichokes with herbs, salmon with lemon sauce, and a cold vegetable soufflé. The pasta course boasts a richly flavoured *tagliolini ai funghi*, scented with cep mushrooms, and tagliolini with an aubergine/eggplant sauce. The main dishes include *carpaccio* (raw sliced beef), *baccalà* (salt fish), a dish of large grilled *funghi porcini*, and deep-fried rabbit. Simple desserts include chocolate tart, lemon tart and crème caramel.

Price: Inexpensive; credit cards not accepted
Closed: Monday
Location: Central Pisa, off Via Francesco

Sergio
Lungarno Pacinotti 1, Pisa
Tel. (050) 48245

Sergio is an elegant, formal restaurant on the banks of the river Arno housed in an historic inn which has offered hospitality to a host of illustrious guests including Shelley, Byron and Garibaldi.

From dire necessity Sergio started his catering career when he was only 13 years old, and for the next 20 years he served a gruelling apprenticeship in many top Italian restaurants. In 1970 he opened his own restaurant for the first time, moving in 1976 to his present site. Today he is president of the Tuscan chefs' society and secretary of the Italian professional restaurateurs.

Sergio loves tradition but he feels free to be creative, and his style of cooking draws on all of the regional variations. He serves small portions of rich ingredients, using herbs very carefully to bring out subtle flavours. As well as an *à la carte* menu, he offers each day three different set menus that are excellent value for money since the prices include appropriate wines, mineral water, coffee, cover and service charges and tax.

The richest menu offers seven courses with four superb wines. Typically, this starts with small savouries, moves on to a delicious lobster salad, followed by black tagliatelle with shrimps in a delicate pumpkin sauce, and a typical Tuscan soup. Between the delicate fish and the rich meat courses Sergio serves a fragrant pink sorbet made with lemon and rose petals. A sumptuous selection of desserts is followed by small home-made sweets. The wines for this menu are Benefizio fattorie Frescobaldi, Schiava di Faedo di Pojer & Sandri, Pulignano 79 fattoria di Bibbiani, and Veruzzo spumante dolce produttori di Cormons.

Price: Moderate to expensive; Amex, Visa
Closed: Sunday, Monday Lunch; January, July 15-28
Location: Beside River Arno at Ponte di Mezzo

San Vincenzo

*S*an Vincenzo, on the Etruscan Riviera coast, is home to one of Italy's most promising young chefs.

Ristorante Gambero Rosso
Piazze della Vittoria 13
Tel. (0565) 701021

Fulvio Pierangelini and his wife, Emanuela, opened their small elegant restaurant facing the sea in 1981. With no formal training, he has today emerged as a bright young star inventing imaginative new dishes that draw appreciative gourmets from all over the world to this small seaside town.

My last lunch here started with prawns served in a sauce of puréed chick peas. The plate was decorated with two or three whole chick peas and a few drops of light pure olive oil. This unlikely combination looked appealing and was quite delicious. After some good stuffed baby squid, I was served an arresting pasta course of fresh black pasta (the pasta dough was coloured with squid ink) formed into ravioli and stuffed with a shellfish mixture. These were quite exceptional and they alone would have justifed my 100 kilometre trip from Siena.

For the main course, I settled for sea bass cooked with rosemary and garlic, although I was sorely tempted by many of the other fish dishes using artichokes or citrus fruits. Fulvio always has a very satisfying choice of desserts, and I enjoyed hot crêpes flavoured with mandarin liqueur, served with orange sorbet and a light sauce.

The wine list is very complete and I particularly liked the Gaia & Rey chardonnay. Fulvio is always happy to introduce new wines to his customers and on his set daily menu drawn up to provide a good introduction to his style of cooking, he suggests appropriate wines. The restaurant is small so be sure to book.

In the summer of 1988 Fulvio and Emanuela opened a simple beach restaurant a few minutes from the main building. *Il Bucaniere* (Tel. (0565) 703387). This attracts a yachting crowd and those who want to eat in the open air or in a more basic setting, where food is less elaborate.

Price: Moderate; Amex, Diners and Visa
Closed: Tuesday; November
Location: On the coast, San Vincenzo, 60 kilometres south of Livorno

Siena

Siena, 68 kilometres from Florence, is probably the most perfectly preserved of all Tuscan cities, a medieval cluster of buildings centred on the magnificent central square, the Piazza del Campo, where the famous horse race, the *Palio*, takes place every July. There are at least two good small restaurants in Siena itself and the journey to Montereggioni, just 15 kilometres away, can provide a very memorable meal in a magnificent setting.

Antica Botteganova
Strada Chiantigiana 29, Siena
Tel. (0577) 284230

This restaurant is outside the city walls of Siena but well worth a visit for its good food and superb wines. As a young man, the owner, Ettore Silvestri, turned his back on the family catering tradition since he hated the idea of the long working hours and total dedication needed for success. Instead, he started up a piano bar which only occupied his evenings. Gradually, however, through working with wines, he became fascinated with good food as well and he decided to restore the old family property and open a restaurant. His wife, Gabriella, nobly took to the kitchen, and their efforts have now been rewarded with success.

Ettore has an amazing wine list, and the cooking preserves the best of Siena's culinary traditions while introducing a pleasing lightness. On Tuesdays and Fridays fish is available in Siena and Ettore prepares a fish menu for his local customers. However, the normal menu is always available and I think this gives the visitor a better idea of Sienese food. A delightful series of antipasti known as 'frivolities', are served before the more serious pasta or soup course, when well-tried favourites include tagliolini with puréed chick peas, risotto with radicchio, and taglierini with lemon sauce. The main course selection offers every sort of meat cooked on a charcoal grill or meat cooked with herbs and wines. One of the most popular dishes for health-conscious customers is rabbit stewed with black olives. There is a traditional dessert made from a favourite family recipe.

Ask Ettore to show you his 'Cantina' and let him help you choose a special wine.

Price: Moderate; Amex, Diners and Visa
Closed: Sunday
Location: ten minutes by taxi from centre

Al Marsili
Via Del Castoro 3, Siena
Tel. (0577) 47154

This calm, elegant restaurant in a fifteenth century building is within easy walking distance of Piazza del Campo and the Duomo. The service is attentive and the menu is always changing to offer new delights to regular customers.

To start with, there are delightful mushroom *crostini* followed by good pasta dishes and risottos based on asparagus, artichokes, *zucchine* or *funghi porcini* according to season. In cooler months they are also served with heavier duck and quail sauces. The second course offers a rich guinea fowl *alla Medici*, Etruscan-style pigeon and a wide choice of good Tuscan meat dishes. For dessert there are home-made fruit tarts made with seasonal fruits, and the wine list contains a good selection of Tuscan wines.

Price: Moderate; Amex, Diners, Diners, Visa
Closed: Monday
Location: Central Siena, close to Piazza del Campo

La Chiusa

Via della Madonna 88, Montefollonica
Tel. (0577) 669 668

This old farmhouse and olive press are perched on a hill-top commanding broad views of the variegated greens of the Tuscan countryside. *La Chiusa* with its comfortable rooms in restored outbuildings invites an overnight stay. I enjoyed breakfast on the terrace outside my room, sampling the home-made bread, cakes and jams, and admiring the scenery in warm May sunshine, almost as much as dinner the previous evening beneath the beamed ceiling and open fireplace of the restaurant.

This Tuscan retreat has been restored by Dania and Umberto Lucherini from a delapidated family property. Dania was a law student in Florence until she met Umberto and moved to Montefollonica. She had grown up in a family that cared about good food and, when she encountered the rather basic rustic fare at *La Chiusa*, she decided that something must be done. Over the years *La Chiusa* has become almost self-sufficient within the community, buying only staples like salt, sugar, milk (for legal reasons) and parmesan cheese elsewhere. Everything else – meat, vegetables and fruit – is provided by neighbouring farmers, working to precise specifications laid down by Umberto. Three local women work in the kitchens preparing the bread, cakes and fresh pasta, and one arrives early each morning to prepare herb breads in the traditional old oven.

The menu naturally changes with the season and you may choose from a wide *à la carte* selection or try the *degustazione* (gastronomic) menu. In spring I began with delicate marrow (squash) flowers stuffed with ricotta cheese and served in a light *zucchini* mousse sauce. Dania also makes good traditional soups using dried beans and peas and whole grains, and her pasta list is an endless temptation. Her risotto is not to be missed if artichokes or *funghi porcini* are in season. The meat courses offers the best of local rabbit, pigeon, duck, guinea fowl and lamb, with beef and veal from the nearby Valdichiana. Do not neglect the pastries, sorbets and icecreams for dessert which come 'signed' by Dania in fragrant fruit sauce.

The wine cellar offers a choice selection of chiantis and the rich Brunello di Montalcino made just a few kilometres away.

Price: Expensive; Amex and Diners
Closed: Tuesday; January
Location: 110 km S. of Florence; 60 km E. of Siena, off S146 to Pienza

Il Pozzo
Piazza Roma 2, Monteriggioni
Tel. (0577) 304127

Monteriggioni is a small fortified village north of Siena, set high on a hill in a strategic position dominating the valley. Completely encircled by surprisingly intact thirteenth century walls, it boasts 14 watch-towers and the remains of a drawbridge. In 'The Inferno', Dante calls Monteriggioni's walls 'a crown'.

Il Pozzo is in the entrance square opposite the old well which gives the restaurant its name. This square provides the only parking in the village, but hopefully there will eventually be a purpose-built car park outside the walls, and *Il Pozzo* will be able to put tables outside in the charming square.

Vittore Franci rules the restaurant while his wife Lucia runs the kitchen. The dining-rooms are warmly welcoming with lovingly displayed fresh fruit and vegetables giving an impression of the style of food – simple but good – making use of first class local produce. To start with there is Tuscan *prosciutto*, a little salty but good with the saltless bread, fennel-flavoured *finocchiona*, and *crostini* and *bruschetta* (savoury toasts). The pasta course offers *papardelle* with a hare or wild boar sauce, *pici* (the local home-made flour and water pasta) and a good bean soup. In the spring I enjoyed a light artichoke risotto. The main course offers good Tuscan beef, grilled lamb or stuffed pigeon and rabbit. On some days there is roe buck and wild boar cooked in a sweet-sour sauce. There is a good trolley of home-made desserts, with the apple tart being especially delicious.

The good selection of Tuscan wines is much appreciated. On my last visit I watched three local businessmen conferring with Vittore as they chose their wine – several bottles – and had it decanted and lined up ready for them to get to.

Price: Moderate; Amex, Diners
Closed: Sunday and Monday lunch. Usually January and August
Location: 15 kilometres NW of Siena, off SS2

La Frateria di Padre Eligio
Convento di S. Francesco, Cetona
Tel. (0578) 238015

This old Francescan monastery dating from the thirteenth century, which had been abandoned in ruins, has been painstakingly restored to its former beauty by the young people working with Padre Eligio in a drug rehabilitation programme called Mondo X. The monastery now has beautiful gardens, complete with helicopter pad, and a few simple but very comfortable bedrooms with private baths for overnight guests. The young people make excellent bread and jams for a delightful breakfast.

The restaurant is elegantly simple and the service is carefully attentive. The wine list, chosen by the expert Veronelli, offers very good wines although they are rather expensive. The cheese, *salame* and olive oil are produced by the neighbouring twin commune and there is an extensive set menu.

For antipasto I enjoyed a light cream of onion tart and a pleasant turkey and pink grapefruit salad. This was followed by a rather substantial borlotti bean risotto and a green peppercorn sorbet. The beef and chicken main course was a little disappointing but there were delectabled desserts and pastries to compensate.

The restaurant offers an unusual dining experience and all the work is carried out by the young Mondo X people. Several top chefs have lent their expertise to this project, and their young disciples work long hours with great dedication to please their customers.

It is essential to book in advance.

Price: Very expensive but the money goes to a good cause, Amex for restaurant, but no cards or official receipt for the bedrooms where payment is regarded as a donation to charity.
Closed: Tuesday and January and February
Location: 50 km S. of Arezzo, A1 exit to Chiusi

~ RECIPE ~

Sformata di Fagiolini e Tonno
Creamed tuna and green beans
from Cibreo, Florence

300 grms/10 oz green French beans
300 grms/10 oz tinned tuna
50 grms/1⅔ oz (3½ tbsp) butter
30 ml/2 tbsp olive oil
1 pinch marjoram, oregano, chopped parsley (fresh)
1 clove garlic

Cook the green beans very lightly in salted water, taking care not to overcook them. Take six small cocottes or ramekins and line the bottom and sides with the green beans. Add all the remaining ingredients to a processor and process to a fine cream. Fill the lined moulds with this mixture which will help to keep the beans in place. Refrigerate for 30 minutes. Turn out onto small plates and anoint with a very little finest quality olive oil before serving.
Serves 4.

GENOA

RECCO

CAMOGLI

PORTOFINO

LEIVI

CHIAVARI

VERNAZZA

PORTOVENERE

TELLARO

AMEGLI

GENOA
& the Ligurian coast

*L*igurian cooking is dominated by the sea. Genoa (known as *La Superba*, the proud) was one of the great maritime republics and for centuries local men depended on the capricious sea for their livelihood and fortune. The mountains come very close to the coastline, leaving only a narrow belt of land to be cultivated, and it took hard toil to carve out vineyards, vegetable plots and building land. Yet Nature smiles on this region, and vegetables, herbs and fruit grow profusely, gaining a distinctive flavour from the perpetual salt winds from the sea. Since pasture land is scarce, meat dishes are few, and the emphasis is on fish, vegetables, herbs and the cep mushrooms called *funghi porcini*, from the mountains of the Apennines.

In the past the women of Genoa often suffered great hardship with their men away at sea for months at a time, so they learned to be ingenious and make interesting dishes with unusual combinations of fairly basic ingredients. The famous Ligurian sauce *pesto* makes use of the readily-available basil, olive oil, cheese and pine nuts or walnuts. Genoese sailors used to take jars of pesto on their long sea voyages to add flavour to the dull ships' rations. Tradition has it that ravioli was invented on board ship by the Genoese. In local dialect, *rabiole* means 'left-overs' and in order to make the most of the food available the left-overs from one meal were chopped up finely and stuffed into little pasta cases to provide the next meal.

In Ligurian cooking everything is stuffed, not only the pasta. Nowadays great care is used in selecting first-class materials to fill vegetables, marrow (squash) flowers, squid, shellfish and meat. The famous dish *cima alla genovese*, is memorable for its stuffing not for the meat casing: a boned breast of veal is used to form a pocket which is then stuffed with a delicious mixture of minced meats, herbs, peas, spinach and pistachio nuts.

Other typical dishes make imaginative use of a few genuinely 'poor' ingredients. The delicious soup, *mesciua*, much prized today, is made from dried beans, chick peas and grain but was invented as a sustaining meal when only a few beans and chick peas were available and there was not enough grain to make bread.

The famous *farinata* made of chick pea flour, olive oil and salt and pepper was once a 'poor', one-dish meal, but today prosperous Genoese trek to the old humble eating-houses where this treat is still cooked in wood-fuelled ovens. *Farinata* can be bought to take away but really it should be eaten as it emerges from the oven in its great flat pan. In Genoa, *farinata* can be sampled with a glass of local wine at the marble tables of *Guglie* in Via S. Vincenzo. Or you might try *Antica Sciamadda* in Via S. Giorgio near Porta Soprana, which was opened over 150 years ago. Much of the original decor remains the same, including the great oven.

The Genoese as a people have always been thrifty and

suspicious of change. Although their ships carried home cargoes of costly spices from the east, the merchants preferred to sell them all for profit and they do not appear in regional cooking. But the Genoese took their cooking traditions away with them. Legend has it that during the Crusades the Genoese contingent could be easily identified by the aroma of *pesto* that surrounded them. In the same Crusades, Goffredo di Buglione handsomely rewarded the men who searched the alien hills for fragrant herbs for his dinner. These little bunches of various herbs became known as *pro Buglione* and it is believed that this is the origin of the name *preboggion*. *Preboggion* is a mixed bunch of herbs, varying according to season, that can be bought in the markets in and around Genoa, to be used in stuffing the famous local pasta *pansoti*.

Torta pasqualina is another example of the Genoese using their imagination to make an economical dish rich and special. Traditionally it was an Easter (*Pasqua*) tart, but it has now become a typical all-the-year treat. A mixture of cheese, hard-boiled eggs, herbs and artichokes or chard is covered by layers of puff pastry. The art lies in the construction of the layered crust. The pastry is rolled out very thinly until it has the texture of tissue paper and then it is lightly brushed with olive oil. (This technique made me wonder if there was an Arab influence here since it seems so similar to filo pastry.) Traditionally, every tart should be covered by 18 or 33 pastry layers, forming a cupola over the filling; old-time cooks used to blow under each layer before sealing it down so that the trapped air kept the pastry domed.

The Genoese *cucina povera* made good use of fried things in the popular tradition of Naples. At one time *friggitorie* (fried food shops) were found all round the port. A few still exist and even good restaurants and homes serve fried vegetables, fish and *funghi porcini*. A Genoese proverb says, *Fritta e buona persino una scarpa*. (Even a shoe tastes good when it is fried).

Cappon Magro is one of the few traditional Ligurian dishes which is unashamedly extravagant. *Magro*, or lean, means without meat in culinary Italian. On days when the Church prohibited meat the rich Ligurians 'mortified' themselves

with a 'lean capon'. The
traditional recipe uses the
galletta, a dried crust made to last
out long sea voyages, as a base, and
piled incredible meatless luxuries on top. This
moistened, seasoned crust is first covered with a variety of
cooked vegtetables cut into strips. These vegetables are then
flavoured by a thick green sauce made from parsley and
anchovies. A new layer is then built up of a variety of very
fine fish and this layer in its turn is covered by the same green
sauce. A layer of sliced artichokes, hard-boiled eggs, olives,
mushrooms and prawns are then arranged,
often topped by a whole lobster and
several dozen oysters!

In Genoa, the sweet-toothed
should visit *Klainguti* in Piazza
Soziglia, a pastry and ice
cream shop opened in 1828
by a Swiss family that had
originally come to Genoa
with the idea of taking a
boat to America. Happily
for Genoa they decided to
stay and soon attracted an
illustrious clientele. Mazzini
was a frequent visitor and Verdi
consumed such a huge quantity of
a certain type of *brioche* that it was
renamed 'Falstaff' in his honour.
Romanengo in Via Orefici is another good
address for delicious cakes. The Genoese eat almost as early
as the French. Lunch can be ordered from 12.30 until 2, and
in the evening it is quite difficult to eat after 10 o'clock.
Visitors inspired to visit the old dock area and its narrow
streets in search of *farinata* should leave valuables and
jewellery in the hotel safe.

Bruxaboschi
Via Mignone 8, Genoa
Tel. (010) 3450302

If you only have time to eat one meal in Genoa, jump into a taxi and visit *Bruxaboschi* which is 6 kilometres from the centre. You feel as if you are in the heart of the country in this welcoming trattoria where you will sample all the inland Ligurian specialities and relax in the warm, family atmosphere.

The trattoria was opened by the present owners' great-grandfather. He had enjoyed a rather wild youth, earning himself the nickname *bruxaboschi* (he who sets fire to the woods), and when he decided to settle down he chose to remember his pecadillos by giving his nickname to his trattoria. The trattoria has always come down through the female side of the family. Maria Giulia, the daughter of the founder, married Angelo Sciaccaluga and carried on the business. Gemma Sciaccaluga in turn inherited *Bruxaboschi* from her parents, and today her two daughters, Ivana and Ada, carry on the family tradition, helped by their husbands and children. Ivana's son, Matteo, although only 17 years old, has an innate flair for cookery and makes beautiful fresh pasta, rolling it out finely with a master's touch. The restaurant is still in its original site amid the green hills of San Desiderio, and in summer months the tables are set outside on the cool, flowery terrace.

Sit and relax with a glass of white Lupi Pigato while you consider your options. For *antipasti* there are vegetables like sweet peppers, onions, zucchine, and aubergines (eggplants) filled with a cheese and herb stuffing and then lightly fried. They are among the best stuffed vegetables I have ever eaten and not to be missed. There are several very interesting pasta dishes such as a green ravioli, made with borage not spinach, stuffed with mushrooms. I also love *piccage matte al pesto*, an old recipe from the *cucina povera* tradition which was evolved to provide sustaining food using cheap, readily-available ingredients. The pasta, made with chestnut flour which the country folk could obtain more easily, is cut up into haphazard strips and cooked together with potatoes and broad beans. When ready the whole mixture is served with a thick *pesto* (see recipe). It is worth following the *antipasti* with a small portion of both these pasta dishes because it is difficult to find them elsewhere.

For the main course, *Bruxaboschi* offers interesting meat and *funghi porcini* dishes, but I suggest contenting yourself with a thin sliver of the tasty stuffed veal dish, *cima genovese* (here prepared with only the best ingredients) in order to be able to do justice to what follows. A rich selection of desserts includes the beautifully-cooked traditional *latte dolce fritto* (fried custard) and *panna cotta* (flavoured cream), flanked by innovations created by Alessandro, Ivana's husband. I have fond memories of his caramelised figs.

A happy trattoria with a rare charm, and it is well worth leaving the centre of Genoa to enjoy a meal here.

Price: Inexpensive to moderate; credit cards not accepted
Closed: Sunday eve, Monday; August
Location: 6 km from city centre, San Desiderio area

Aladino
Via Ettore Vernazza 8, Genoa
Tel. (010) 566788

Aladino is a quiet, civilised restaurant in the centre of Genoa with a large clientele of businessmen and politicians who appreciate the comfortable distance between the tables and the smooth, discreet service. The restaurant is welcoming in the cool months and the air conditioning is a boon during the summer heat.

The brothers Franco and Lino Alessi who own *Aladino* came from Calabria in the south, but they have spent years in Genoa and their menu carries all the local specialities. To begin there is a modest version of the opulent *cappon magro* and in season a soup of tiny fish, *bianchetti*. There is also a variation on the usual prosciutto and melon where wild boar ham, *cinghiale*, is served with fresh ripe figs. The pasta dishes are all very good, but I particularly recommend homemade taglierini.

For the main course there is tasty *stoccafisso* – the local way of cooking dried cod introduced into Liguria by sailors returning from voyages in the north – or simply-cooked fresh fish such as *branzino* (sea bass) or *orata* (bream). The swordfish (*pesce spada*) speciality consists of cubes of swordfish cooked very quickly in olive oil with chopped *funghi porcini*, an unusual combination but very good.

A selection of desserts includes the Ligurian *latte dolce fritto* and an interesting chestnut pudding.

Among the good choice of wines I suggest a Pigato di Albenga to go with the fish and a Dolceacqua to accompany meat.

Price: Moderate to expensive; Amex, Diners, Visa
Closed: Sunday
Location: central Genoa

Cicchetti 1860

Via Gianelli 41 (Quinto), Genoa
Tel. (010) 331641

Quinto, five Roman milestones from the centre of Genoa, used to be inhabited mainly by fishermen and dockers when Angelo Penco opened his osteria here in 1860. For a very moderate sum the men could enjoy a bowl of Genoese minestrone soup and a glass of wine. A *cicchetto*, the equivalent of the modern *bicchierino* (a small glass of spirits), was drunk to give energy for the hard work and the long walk to Genoa, and since Angelo shared his customers' enjoyment the osteria became known as *Cicchetti*.

After the First World War, Quinto began to attract more elegant visitors from Genoa and they loved the simple food of the humble osteria with its enticing aromas. Angelo's son, Rinaldo, enlarged the menu to include fresh fish and other Ligurian specialities and in the kitchen, visible from the restaurant, the women of the family, Giulia and Carlotta, worked endlessly making fresh pasta and pounding basil for *pesto*.

Today Renato Rovani, an ex-waiter, continues the *Cicchetti* tradition. Physically, the restaurant has remained exactly the same; there is a counter near the entrance serving *cicchetti* and the women can still be observed as they work in the kitchen. Many of the staff have worked here all their lives and the menu lists all the traditional dishes. The antipasto is stuffed vegetables and this is followed by lasagne with *pesto* or *minestrone genovese*. For the main course there is a good selection of fresh fish dishes or the more humble *stoccafisso* (dried cod), or *seppie in umido con patate* (stewed squid and potatoes). There is a small selection of home-made desserts, and the meal is rounded off with one more inevitable *cicchetto*, or little drink.

Cicchetti is always full so it is necessary to reserve a table in advance. The regular clientele enjoy the good value for money and the casual visitor enjoys a genuine meal in an atmosphere of 'old Genoa'.

Price: Inexpensive; credit cards not accepted
Closed: August and Tuesday
Location: 8 kilometres south on S1

Rina
Mura delle Grazie, 3, Genoa
Tel. (010) 207990

Rina is in the middle of the *centro storico* (the old centre) very near the port, where the early, pre-Roman settlers founded the city. At the beginning of the century this restaurant was the site of a wine shop providing simple food to satisfy the needs of customers around the port. In 1945, Rina Rapetti took over and within 10 years, *Rina* had become famous as a restaurant serving good fresh fish and local specialities. A faithful following of customers now meets under the low, vaulted ceiling and the good food and simple, unpretentious surroundings seem equally attractive to the long-haired young and the white-haired regulars. Rina herself, at 76, remains an indomitable force while her daughters-

in-law and grand-daughters provide very able assistance.

The house wine is a light, pleasant Gavi but the usual Ligurian wines are also available. The antipasti is a mixture of shellfish or fried stuffed vegetables, a Ligurian speciality. Since this is a fish restaurant *Rina's* speciality is spaghetti with large clams (*vongole veraci*), but I love their light home-made lasagne served with *pesto*. Fish for the main course are brought out on large platters to be inspected by the customer and the chosen fish is cooked to order very simply in the oven (*al forno*) or on the grill. A small selection of homely desserts and good fresh fruit completes the meal.

It is essential to reserve a table because this famous local institution, although large, is always full at lunch and dinner alike.

Price: Moderate; Amex
Closed: Monday
Location: Close to the old port

Antica Osteria del Bai
Via Quarto 12, Genoa (Quarto)
Tel. (010) 387478

This restaurant is a fascinating mixture of past and present. In 1860, Garibaldi ate here before embarking from the beach below with his glorious *mille* – the thousand volunteers – to fight in Sicily for a unified Italy. Various portraits of Garibaldi adorn the walls of the restaurant and a pasta dish *alla garibaldina* made with red mullet (*triglie*), evokes the red shirts of his followers.

The *Antica Osteria* is now owned by Gianni and Renata Malagoli and although they have preserved the original old inn as an entrance they have added a large, luminous veranda built out over the beach and created a very good wine cellar downstairs where the fishermen once stored their boats.

Today, the menu is based mainly on interesting combinations of fish and fresh vegetables and there are some unusual antipasti like lobster and melon salad or shrimps and asparagus tips in a lemon dressing. Gianni originally came from Emilia, famous for its egg pasta, and I find it difficult to choose between his delicate ravioli stuffed with fish and the delicious tortelli with asparagus and black truffles. Ligurian pasta specialities such as *troffiette al pesto* (basil sauce) and *pansoti con salsa di noci* (walnut sauce) are equally good and there are other pasta and risotto dishes which vary according to the season.

For the main course it is possible to select fish, meat or *funghi porcini*, but with the sea lapping round it would seem churlish to pass up *filetto di rombo con asparagi* (halibut with asparagus) or *pesce spada* (swordfish).

A good choice of desserts prepared from fresh fruits in season offers light dishes like peaches in wine jelly or raspberry tart.

The wine list is very complete with a small selection of French wines and wines from all regions of italy. If you have already tried a number of good Ligurian wines I would recommend a white wine from Friuli like Schiopetto's Sauvignon or Tocai.

Price: Moderate to expensive; Amex
Closed: Mondays and March 1-10, July 20-August 10, but check
Location: 7 kilometres from Genoa on S1 towards Rapallo

La Bitta
Via S. Martino, 13, Genoa
Tel. (010) 311052

San Martino, once a resort area, has now been swallowed up by urban development. In the midst of this, *La Bitta*, which opened three years ago, has acquired a devoted following of local 'regulars'.

Raffaelle Balzano used to work as a chef on the great ocean liners but several years ago he decided to use his expertise in a restaurant of his own. He and his wife, Rosa, both from Naples, opened a typical Neapolitan trattoria in Genoa, 'Bella Napoli'. Once the restaurant was firmly established they handed it over to their older children and started *La Bitta* where they draw freely from the culinary traditions of both Naples and Genoa. Although they use the best fresh fish and vegetables from the local markets to make dishes like *gnocci al sugo di aragosta* gnocchi with lobster sauce) or *pesce spada ai funghi porcini* (swordfish with ceps), the spaghetti and linguine are bought from a small artisan factory near Naples, and Rosa scours Neapolitan markets for the small round red tomatoes which grow best on the soil created by the lava from Vesuvius. Even the desserts show the same mixed heritage – the traditional *pastiera* from Naples jostles for a place on the menu with the Genoese *panna cotta*.

Price: Inexpensive to moderate; credit cards not accepted
Closed: Tuesday; part of August
Location: San Martino area

Recco

*A*mere 23 kilometres from central Genoa, Recco has long been recognised as a convenient and interesting gastronomic centre.

Manuelina
Via Roma 278, Recco
Tel. (0185) 74128

Manuelina is one of the most interesting trattorias in Liguria with a fascinating history. First opened by Emanuela (Manuelina) Capurro in 1885 as a staging post, where she offered carters peasant food, local wine and a place to talk and play cards, it gradually became the local eating place for farmers attending cattle fairs and for the seafaring men of neighbouring Camogli who wanted to celebrate their safe return to hearth and family. Manuelina's reputation was made when she invented the delicious *focaccia al formaggio* – a thin pizza-like crust covered with local cheese and baked in a wood oven. Her fame spread and she was discovered by fashionable Ligurian society. It became chic to drive out from Genoa after the theatre or an elegant ball to Recco to eat Manuelina's *focaccia*, and partygoers would rap on her shutters to wake her up so that she could satisfy their craving. Over the years she continued to enjoy great success and the famous came to eat her food, including Mussolini, despite his notoriously poor digestion.

During the last war, the original restaurant building was destroyed, but in 1960 *Manuelina* was re-opened by her granddaughter, Maria Rosa, and her husband, Gianni Carbone, who run the restaurant. Recco is now known as a gastronomic centre

and all the local trattorias advertise *focaccia* as their star attraction. The new *Manuelina* still offers every diner this crispy treat – trolleys containing a sizzling *focaccia* straight from the oven are wheeled from table to table – but the main menu is an interesting mixture of old and new.

Two set menus offer good value for money, and a large *à la carte* selection varies according to season and the local market produce. This is one of the very few Ligurian restaurants to offer the famous local speciality *cappon magro* as an antipasto, although the everyday version is obviously less elaborate than the formal party piece. The *cappon magro* was invented in the distant past to satisfy indulgent Ligurians who wanted to obey the letter of the law, though not the spirit, during the meat-less days decreed by the Church. This is the richest *magro* dish I know in Italian cooking and certainly entails no fasting or hardship. The traditional recipe used the *galletta*, a dried crust made to last out long sea voyages, as a base, and piled incredible meat-less luxuries on top. This moistened, seasoned crust is covered with a variety of cooked vegetables cut into strips. These vegetables are then flavoured by a thick green sauce made from parsley and anchovies. A new layer is then built up of a variety of very fine fish and this layer in its turn is covered by the same green sauce. A layer of sliced artichokes, hard-boiled eggs, olives, mushrooms and prawns are then arranged on top and, as a crowning glory, this creation is topped by a whole lobster and several dozen oysters!

The pasta course here is rich and varied: there are the traditional *trofie al pesto* (basil sauce) and *pansotti alla salsa di noci* (walnut sauce), fettuccine made black by small squid and their ink, and *lasagne al corallo* with a rich, orange, fish sauce. One of the local specialities is fresh pasta cut into rounds – *corzetti*. The wooden cutter is carved with various designs and, for special occasions, the pasta is personalised with a name or special emblem carved on the cutter. *Corzetti* is usually served with a mushroom sauce.

The main course selection has excellent fish but also very good meat dishes which is not always the case in Liguria. Veal with artichokes is highly recommended, and there is very good *pré salé* lamb, imported from France.

To finish the meal there are the usual sorbets and puddings, but I adore *bianco mangiare*, a sort of cream made from almonds, topped by a fresh raspberry sauce.

Manuelina has a superb wine list which contains wines from the whole of Italy, as well as France and California. However, in this most Ligurian of restaurants, it would seem a pity not to drink one of the excellent Ligurian whites such as Pigato, Alessandri or Cinque Terre Cru de Sera. The Ligurian red Rossese di Dolceacqua is also very good.

Manuelina is the perfect antidote to too many indistinguishable fish meals along the coast and here you can realise the full versatility of traditional Ligurian cooking.

Price: Moderate to expensive; Visa, Amex, Diners
Closed: Wednesday; January 12 to February 12, July 20 to 30
Location: 1 km north on the Via Roma

~ RECIPE ~

Piccage matte al Pesto
Chestnut Pasta with Basil Sauce from Bruxaboschi

100g/3½ oz fresh broad (*fava*) beans, shelled
50 g/scant 2 oz potatoes, cut into small cubes
PASTA
225 g/8 oz (1⅔ cups) strong bread flour
75 g/2½ oz (½ cup) chestnut flour (*farina di castagne*)
2 eggs, pinch of salt
little tepid water
PESTO
36 basil leaves (at least 6 per person)
3 cloves garlic
150 g/5 oz (1⅔ cups) pine nuts
100 g/3½ oz (1¼ cups) freshly grated mixed
Pecorino romano and Parmesan cheese
200 ml/7 oz good quality olive oil
salt and freshly ground black pepper

Mix the white and chestnut flours together and make a well in the centre; add the eggs and salt. Mix into a smooth dough, adding a little tepid water if necessary. Roll out the pasta dough thinly and cut into strips. Bring a large pan of salted water to the boil. Add the pasta strips, beans and potatoes and cook for approximately 15 minutes, testing to make sure that they are not overdone. Meanwhile, wipe the basil leaves with a damp cloth and place them in a food processor, together with the cloves of garlic. Turn on the processor and gradually add the nuts, then the cheese and olive oil. Season to taste. Drain the pasta, potatoes and beans, reserving 15-30 ml/1-2 tablespoons of the cooking water to add to the pesto. Arrange the pasta, potatoes and beans in a large bowl. Stir the pesto into this mixture. Serve immediately. Serves 4.

Camogli

*I*n local dialect *'Ca' 'Mogli'* means 'the home of the wives' and the town grew up as a sailors' settlement where the wives patiently awaited the men's return.

Ristorante Rosa
Largo Casabona 11, Camogli
Tel. (0815) 771088

Rosa's splendid terrace is perched right on the edge of the cliff just outside Camogli. Lunchtime customers can look down to the cool blue rocky sea or across to the colourful houses grouped round the small port.

Rosa opened in 1949 as a pensione run by Nonna Rosa, grandmother of the present owners, and Zio Ettore who was a ship's cook during the First World War. Now it is a restaurant without rooms, specialising in seafood and local pasta specialities. The choice of fish inevitably depends on the local catch, but there are always shellfish like *datteri*, *cozze* and *vongole* kept alive in filtered, sea water tanks. The *zuppa di datteri* (sea-date soup) is very good, but the fresh pasta made by the local women is exquisite. Here *pansotti alla salsa di noci* (pasta with walnut sauce) is deliciously aromatic and slightly different from the usual Ligurian recipe, since Maria Rosa, grand-daughter of the founder, adds freshly grated nutmeg to the herb stuffing and her walnut sauce contains no garlic. *Lasagne al pesto* consists of three large, thin squares of pasta spread with *pesto*, piled one on top of the other. The pasta is rolled out until it is very fine (known in dialect as silk handkerchiefs). The full flavour of the basil sauce shows to greater advantage with this pasta than with the short, thick *troffie* made by hand with flour and water.

With its good selection of local wines, *Rosa* is to be recommended as an oasis of calm after the frenetic confusion of nearby Portofino in the throes of its summer invasion.

Price: Moderate; Amex
Closed: Tuesday; February 15 to 26, November 2-December 16
Location: 26 kilometres south of Genoa S1

Portofino

Portofino is still beautiful. The coastal road can become very congested during the high season and in the heat of the day the main parking square becomes an inferno, but the harbour is closed to traffic and remains unspoiled. The small, deeply-indented natural harbour is encircled by painted houses set against a backcloth of lush green woods studded with interesting castles and churches. Nowadays glittering yachts and colourful small boats sport in the deep blue waters that were once the domain of the playful dolphins who gave the port its name – portus Delphini.

Il Pitosoforo
Via Molo Umberto, 9, Portofino
Tel. (0185) 269020

I find this an enchanting restaurant. The dining-room is reached by a flight of steps and the window-side tables make you feel as if you are in a box at the opera. During dinner the restaurant lights are turned off for a few minutes so that the full beauty of the illuminated stage-set of the harbour can be appreciated.

The restaurant gets its name from the pitosoforo tree which grows up through the restaurant roof. *Il Pitosoforo* was owned for over 30 years by Marco Vinelli and he played host to the famous who visited Portofino in their yachts. In 1988, the restaurant changed hands and the menu suggested by the new owners is shorter but quite pleasing.

Fresh fish dominates, but the traditional Ligurian pasta with *pesto* or walnut sauce also appear on the menu and both are good. The lobster and scampi looked enticing but I settled for a large *branzino* (bass) encased in sea salt and baked in a hot oven.

The desserts did not seem very inspired but there was a very good selection of fresh fruit and an apple sorbet topped with calvados.

The wine list is very long and clearly designed to satisfy the most demanding palate but most would be pleased with a local wine. Vermentino or Pigato goes very well with the fish.

Price: Expensive; Amex, Diners, Visa
Closed: Tuesday, Wednesday lunch
Location: 36 kilometres south of Genoa; by harbour

Puny

Piazza Oliveyya 7, Portofino
Tel. (0185) 269037

When you eat at one of the outside tables *da Puny* you feel as if you have a ring-side seat. The trattoria has an enviable position right on the little piazza fronting the harbour and this piazza is the hub of Portofino life. Order a bottle of chilled Cinque Terre, Vermentino or Pigato (local Ligurian white wines) and sit back to enjoy the spectacle.

Luigi Miroli – known as 'Puny' – opened his trattoria in 1980, but he grew up in this environment. His grandmother, Santa, started the first trattoria in 1880 and since then all the family have been involved.

Puny is enjoyed by Italians and foreigners alike. The seafood is fresh and well-cooked and all the local pasta specialities can be found here, including the non-fish *pasta al pesto* (with basil sauce) and *pansotti alla salsa di noci* (with walnut sauce).

For the main course I suggest *fritto di calamari e gamberi* – rings of squid and prawns dipped in a light batter and fried, or a whole fish baked in a crust of sea salt. This method seals in all the flavour and is very light as no oil is used. If you feel like a more decisive flavour order the fish with *guazzetto*, a sauce based on tomatoes. The desserts are very simple variations on fruit and icecream.

Price: *Moderate to expensive; credit cards not accepted*
Closed: *Thursday; January 2 to March 2*
Location: *Harbour front*

Chiavari

Chiavari was important in the past for its strategic position on the coast (*chiave* means 'key'), but now, in tourist terms, it has been rather over-shadowed by its better-known neighbours, Rapallo and Santa Margherita. This makes Chiavari rather more interesting, gastronomically-speaking.

Copetin
Piazza Gagliardo 16, Chiavari
Tel. (0185) 309064

In a quiet square just off the sea-front there is a delightful little fish restaurant frequented for the most part by Italians in search of good food and wine. The buildings of the piazza, over 400 years old, used to be fishermen's cottages, and the restaurant owners, Alda Nidielli and Franco Conti, have skilfully created two small elegant dining-rooms from one cottage, exposing the original beamed ceilings, and in the summer months tables are set outside in the peaceful square.

The menu varies according to the daily catch, and if the sea has been ungenerous the restaurant remains closed rather than compromise with inferior ingredients. This happens very rarely but it is worth phoning in advance to make sure. The antipasti, risotto and pasta dishes are all exclusively fish, so do not expect to find *pesto* or walnut sauce. However, the fish is cooked in a myriad of different ways and variety is achieved by flavouring the fish with pine nuts, or *guazzetto* a green sauce made from a mixture of onions, tomatoes and pine nuts. Particularly recommended are the grilled slices of swordfish where the fine natural flavour needs only a squeeze of fresh lemon.

Alda is a professional cook but her husband, Franco, used to be in the insurance business. However, he happily left insurance 13 years ago to help his wife open the restaurant and he has become an expert sommelier. *Copetin* has an excellent wine list and Franco will happily help you to choose a fine local wine like a Vermentino or Pigato.

The name *Copetin* has interesting origins. At night small fishing boats used strong lights – *lampara* – to attract the fish to the surface to be caught. The old-fashioned *lampara*, fuelled by acetylene, grew very hot and the fishermen took advantage of this to cook themselves a tasty meal. They brought a simple tomato sauce from home in a little metal cup (*copetin*) and freshly-caught anchovies were cooked in this sauce when the cups were placed on the hot lamps.

Price: Moderate to expensive, Amex, Diners
Closed: Tuesday evening and Wednesday; December and January
Location: Near sea front

~ RECIPE ~

Latte Dolce Fritto
Fried Cream Custards
from Il Gambero Rosso, Vernazza

6 egg yolks
125 g/4 oz sugar
50 g/1⅔ oz (6 tbsp) cornflour (cornstarch)
500 ml/16 fl oz (2 cups) milk
grated zest of 1 lemon
1 vanilla pod (bean)
1 egg white
oil for deep frying
very fine fresh breadcrumbs
icing sugar (confectioner's) for dusting

Mix the egg yolks very carefully with the sugar and cornflour. In a saucepan, boil the milk with the vanilla. Cool the milk to just below boiling, then add, stirring all the time, to the egg yolk and sugar mixture. When smooth add the lemon zest and remove the vanilla pod. Cook this egg custard for 45 minutes very gently in a bain-marie (or with the saucepan sitting in another pan of boiling water). Stir constantly so that the custard thickens without forming lumps. (If lumps do form the whole custard can be quickly rectified by blending or processing.) Pour the very thick custard into a shallow rectangular tin that has been greased and lined with baking parchment. Leave overnight to set.

Whisk the egg white until frothy, and heat a pan of deep oil for frying. Slice the thick custard into squares, dip in the egg white and then into the breadcrumbs. Fry in hot oil for 2-3 minutes. The outside of these little *dolci* should be crisp and the inside soft and creamy. Dust with sugar and serve.
Serves 4.

Ca' Peo
Via dei Caduti, 80, Leivi
Tel. (0185) 319090

Ca' Peo does not cater for the spur-of-the-moment diner. You must reserve a table at least a day in advance. However, if you are in the area it is well worth making the trip here to sample the best of Ligurian gastronomy.

Melly and Franco Solari are perfectionists and in their small, elegant restaurant high in the hills, 6 kilometres above Chiavari, they shop and cook for each customer with the same care a gourmet host lavishes on a small, special dinner party. Leivi, half an hour's drive from Portofino, enjoys a panoramic view of the coastline and in this peaceful, rural setting the Solaris provide superb food and wine and also warm hospitality for any guest who plans to spend the night in one of their comfortable bedrooms.

For generations, Franco's family have eked out a living on this land. When Franco started working in local restaurants he discovered a passion for good food and wine. After he had learned all he could from many great restaurants at home and abroad, he returned to Leivi and gradually converted his grandfather, Pietro's small holding into a beautiful, unusual restaurant. (*Ca' Peo* in local dialect means Pietro's house.) In the beginning Franco

planned the menus and did the shopping and his wife, Melly, from Treviso, did the cooking while her husband looked for a good, professional chef. However, Melly revealed great natural talent as she followed her husband's suggestions. Their ecstatic customers made them realise that they made an inspired team. Today, Franco still makes the daily trip to the local markets to select the best ingredients and Melly with his advice turns them into magical feasts.

Melly, like all great masters, makes everything seem effortless. One late afternoon I remember seeing her sitting relaxed on her kitchen terrace with two replete cats dozing among the flowers, shelling broad beans as if she had no care in the world. Two hours later I was eating the same beans transformed into a delectable, subtle terrine.

The menu uses all the good local produce as it comes into season. In late spring asparagus spears are wrapped in airy crêpes and the *funghi porcini* for which the region is famous appear in many guises. I still remember a main course of crisp *funghi porcini*, dipped in a very light batter and then quickly fried. Many traditional dishes appear on the menu, such as *lattughe ripiene in brodo* (lettuce stuffed with a meat mixture and cooked in broth to make a nourishing soup) or *tomaxelle* (fine slices of veal stuffed with a mixture of meat, nuts and herbs, then rolled up and cooked in a thin tomato sauce). These humble dishes stand side by side with more extravagant rack of lamb, lobster or foie gras. Franco lovingly guides you through the menu suggesting a judicious selection of homely and sophisticated cooking which go surprisingly well together. The desserts are simple but I particularly enjoy melon mousse, caramelised orange segments, or apple flambé with grapes, pine nuts and chestnut ice cream.

Franco has a great selection of Italian and French wines in his cellar under the dining-room where the old olive oil press used to be housed. However, he has a very good choice of Ligurian wines and in order to encourage regional wine producers to develop their potential, 6 years ago he inaugurated an annual prize – *Ronseggin d'Ou* to be awarded to the Ligurian vineyard which has made the most progress during the year.

Ca' Peo is an experience not to be missed for those who are seriously interested in good food and wine.

Price: Moderate to expensive; Visa
Closed: Monday and Tuesday lunch; January 11 to February 5 and November 7-30
Location: 6 kilometres N from Chiavari

Cinque Terre

*T*he Cinque Terre, or 'five lands', are five small fishing villages clustered precariously between Portovenere and Levanto where the Appenine ridges come right down to the sea. These communities began in the Middle Ages and over the centuries, with back-breaking toil, the local inhabitants have established terraced vineyards on the almost vertical hills. Today Cinque Terre wine is generally appreciated but even in the Middle Ages Boccaccio and Petrarch sang its praises.

Gambero Rosso

Piazza Marconi 16, Vernazza
Tel. (0187) 812265

The *Gambero Rosso* is a good place for lunch. The main dining-room is partly a grotto carved from the rock, very cool in summer. However, when the trattoria is busy it tends to be noisy and it is perhaps preferable to eat outside in the little piazza beside the harbour.

The restaurant serves a local wine in a jug, but I prefer the D.O.C. Cinque Terre. I suggest you skip the antipasto and start your meal with the very good *troffie al pesto* – thick, short pasta made by hand or with fresh ravioli stuffed with fish. This can be followed either by an unusual local speciality, *tian vernazza*, made from anchovies, potatoes and tomatoes, or a plate of stuffed mussels, another local speciality.

Dessert is worth ordering as an excuse to enjoy a glass of the legendary Sciacchetra – the local sweet wine. This wine is produced in limited quantity and local families lay it down for their children when they are born. Traditionally the bottles are buried in the sand to mature at a constant temperature. At the very end of the meal the D'Ambra family offer every guest a delicious sweet called *latte dolce fritte*. To make this, a thick egg custard is poured on to a shallow tray and allowed to cool, then cut into small shapes, rolled in egg white and fine breadcrumbs and deep fried. I found it so delicious I begged for the recipe.

Price: Inexpensive; credit cards not accepted
Closed: Monday; February, November 1-20
Location: Twisty side-road off S1, N of La Spezia, or boat

Portovenere

Portovenere was once a naval base where the Romans kept their triremes ready for voyages to Gaul. During the Middle Ages Portovenere became a small Genoese colony and the narrow alleys running behind the long quay with its colourful terraced houses date from this era. Although a new road has been built to give greater access to the coast line, Portovenere still remains a charming little village. However, sea-front trattorias have mushroomed and it is best to be selective and not too influenced by the view.

La Medusa

Via Capellini 74, Portovenere
Tel. (0187) 900603

La Medusa is in the narrow, medieval Via Capellini next to a little piazza with an attractive old well. The chef-owner, Ermes, is originally from Milan but he has worked all over Europe, and he and his Swedish wife, Ulla, used to have a restaurant in Spain, near Alicante. He serves all the local Ligurian specialities but occasionally there are certain interesting variations, inspired by his wide culinary experience. The antipasto is a veritable feast,

and as we were quickly surrounded by a series of small terracotta dishes until the table overflowed, I was reminded of the Spanish *tapas* tradition.

The house wine, a delicious Vermentino Lunae from nearby Castelnuovo Magra, is dry with a slight tingle – it is very enjoyable and disappears very quickly. The *Zuppa di datteri* (sea date soup) is good but I was intrigued by a very unusual *penne agli scampi*. I could not identify the extra flavour anld I was even more mystified when told 'curry', since the taste was not hot and had nothing in common with any combination of spices I have heard described as 'curry'. However, whatever the explanation, the dish was excellent and not to be missed.

As in most fish restaurants, the second course depends on the local catch. Good desserts and a home-made lemon liqueur make a fitting end to a very enjoyable meal. Most of the other customers always seem to be locals and lunch here is like being part of the close-knit community.

Price: Moderate; credit cards not accepted
Closed: Monday
Location: 12 km from La Spezia

Lerici

*W*ithin easy distance of Lerici, a small fishing port on the gulf of La Spezia, are three attractive restaurants, one of which is now renowned internationally.

Locanda dell 'Angelo
Viale 25 Aprile, Ameglia
Tel. (0187) 64391

Angelo Paracucchi, originally from Umbria – a region famous for its good food – began working in restaurants 40 years ago. Today he is the doyen of the new Italian cooking and he is constantly on the move between France where he has a restaurant, Seoul where he is in the process of opening a restaurant, Japan where he has set up a franchise of 'Eating Corners', and the United States where he teaches Italian culinary arts. However, he is mostly found in his modern, purpose-built restaurant at Ameglia, just outside Lerici and the beautiful Ligurian coast.

The restaurant is elegant but unpretentious like Angelo

himself who feels happiest in his simple white chef's coat as he greets each new guest, explaining the day's menu and making suggestions. Angelo places the utmost importance on good quality basic ingredients. He himself is meticulous in choosing the *materia prima* at just the right moment and he has trained his staff to do the marketing with the same discerning eye. He prefers to work with fillets rather than whole fish so that portions can be cooked quickly for each individual order. The local vegetables are chosen carefully as they come into season and cooked with the same light hand and precision timing. Judicious use is made of *funghi porcini* when they are at their best, and Angelo's Umbrian birthright is revealed in superb black truffle dishes. The meat dishes are equally subtle and there is a rich selection of desserts.

The extensive wine list makes interesting reading and the staff are always happy to suggest the right wines to enhance your chosen menu.

Angelo is a very creative cook and presents a menu that is always changing with 10 or so items to choose from for each course. The antipasti contain some luxury items given a novel twist, like *carpaccio* (wafer-thin raw beef) with black truffles and some apparently simple dishes like fillets of *cernia* (a white fish) in a tantalising tomato and thyme sauce that I have tried in vain to copy.

Main courses are always of a consistently high quality with fish dishes such as fillets of sea bass served with a lemon peel crust or fillets of halibut served with an *aceto balsamico* (aromatic vinegar) sauce. The meat course includes local dishes like lamb and artichokes as well as a delicate dish of duck breast with a sauce of mixed citrus fruits. Italian desserts are often rather disappointing but here there is an impressive array and several lush flambé creations.

The menu is balanced with such finesse that the diner does not feel surfeited at the end of the feast.

During February, Angelo holds several one-week residential cooking courses which are geared to enthusiasts at various levels of expertise. The places are limited and have to be booked several months in advance. During the rest of the year, Angelo has several rather severe but very comfortable bedrooms for overnight guests, and breakfast includes very good home-made jams.

Price: Expensive; Visa, Amex, Diners
Closed: January 10 to 31st
Location: 3 km from Ameglia, on the road to Sarzona-Marilenna

Miranda
Via Fiascherino 92, Tellaro
Tel. (0187) 968130

This is one of my favourite Ligurian restaurants. A few years ago, making my way back to Rome in the heat of the summer, thoughts of the sea became irresistible and I decided to leave the traffic of the *autostrada* for a swim and a simple meal on *Miranda*'s cool terrace. To my surprise I found that the unpretentious trattoria I had known for years, had experienced a sea-change and acquired a menu full of intriguing innovations. Nowadays I leave the *autostrada* for an exciting meal at *Miranda* and the sea takes second place, even though it is the beautiful Golfo dei Poeti.

Miranda, the present owners' aunt, used to rent out rooms to passing visitors and this evolved naturally over the years into a pensione and a modest trattoria. When Giovanna and Angelo Cabani took charge Angelo amused himself by inventing a few new recipes, but he became quite irritated when local rivals copied his successful ideas. He threw himself into a frenzy of experiments and, with his great natural flair, he perfected a highly personal style of cooking, very difficult to imitate.

The unwritten menu changes frequently but begins with a series of eight different antipasti. On my last visit I remember thin slices of salmon served with *zucchine* vinaigrette, scampi omelette with a white truffle sauce, lobster and bean salad with a radicchio vinaigrette, little toasts topped with a pâté of salt cod.

The pasta courses are delicious, but I usually go straight on to the main course because the antipasti are like a meal in itself. Fillets of delicate sea bass are tempting but so is an unusual combination of fish with a red wine sauce. Desserts are all very light, like my favourite raspberry mousse or the hot pear tart served with *zabaglione*.

There is a very extensive wine list but I usually ask Giovanna to suggest some discovery. Since the Cabanis are passionately involved with their restaurant, there is always something new.

Price: *Moderate to expensive; Diners*
Closed: *Monday*
Location: *4 km SE from Lerici*

155

Armanda
Piazza Garibaldi 6, Castelnuovo Magra
Tel. (0187) 674410

Castelnuovo Magra is a small medieval village perched in the hills high above Lerici. Dante once stayed here. It is not the sort of place you find by chance; however, knowledgeable Italians happily forsake the coast in order to eat at *Armanda*'s.

This simple, unpretentious one-room trattoria makes no effort to be visually appealing. There is a splendid view outside and permission to make a terrace has been applied for, but bureaucracy moves slowly and in the foreseeable future nothing will change. There are only 20 places and they are always full so it is essential to book in advance.

The trattoria was opened in 1908 by Armanda's grandfather and she grew up absorbing the tradition of good cooking. Today her son, Valerio, the wine expert, serves in the dining-room while his mother, an energetic, down-to-earth woman, cooks local specialities and her own imaginative variations. Her menus are based on good basic ingredients as they come into season and everything is prepared fresh for each customer. The home-made pasta dough is prepared in advance but it is not rolled out, cut or stuffed until the customer has placed his order. Here you eat inspired home-cooking with no professional shortcuts or flourishes. Armanda leaves fish cooking to the coast and concentrates on vegetable and meat dishes. In season she serves game and the exquisite local *funghi porcini*.

The meal starts with local *salame* and a series of delicious hot antipasti, based on the vegetables in season. I have fond memories of asparagus spears wrapped in a light flour and water pancake, spinach tart, stuffed onions and a lovely asparagus terrine. The pasta course is equally good and I especially recommend fresh ravioli stuffed with pumpkin.

The main course usually includes lamb, stuffed rabbit or pork, but I find these rather hearty after the rich selection of antipasti. I usually settle for a light dessert like *panna cotta* with caramel.

Valerio has a good selection of Italian wines but ask him to choose you a good local wine to enhance your Ligurian meal. Amazingly good value.

Price: *Inexpensive; credit cards not accepted*
Closed: *Wednesday*
Location: *3 km off S1 at Molicciara*

Forte Dei Marmi

*T*he Tuscan coastline just before Liguria is not very interesting and one resort seems to run into another with no visible difference. The coast road is flanked by straight, sandy beaches and endless rows of restaurants which all look rather alike.

Maitò
Viale Repubblica, Forte dei Marmi
Tel. (0584) 80840

Maitò, where the food is consistently good and the service quietly attentive, provides a very relaxing escape from the traffic of the hot *autostrada* and a chance to relax on the cool, peaceful terraces of this long-established restaurant.

There are good antipasti comprising shrimps, baby squid, tomatoes, green beans and rocket (arugula) and delicious pasta dishes made from combinations of shellfish and seasonal vegetables like tagliolini with prawns and asparagus tips. For those who prefer just shellfish there is a very delicate dish of pasta cooked with clams, prawns and small squid where it is possible to distinguish the different flavour of each ingredient.

The selection of fresh fish depends on the local market, but I recommend *rombo* (halibut) cooked in the oven with tomatoes and potatoes. *Maitò* serves pizza at lunch as well as dinner and their pizza is famous all along the coast. This must also be the only restaurant in Italy to employ a woman to make the pizza. Traditionally, *pizzalaio* are always male but Mary took over one evening when the usual man was ill and she proved such a success she was asked to continue with her light, crisp inventions.

The local small wild berries – *frutti di bosco* – are very good and there is a traditional tart made with pinenuts called *torta della nonna*, grandmother's tart.

Price: Moderate; Amex, Diners, Visa
Closed: Wednesday
Location: 41 km S of La Spezia

TURIN
& Piedmont

*T*urin is an elegant city with wide porticoed streets running into vast historic squares. The centre has preserved the rectangular shape and parallel roads of the original Roman *castrum* or fort. Turin was dominated by the royal House of Savoy for over nine centuries, culminating in Vittorio Emanuele II becoming the first king of Italy in 1861, and the ruling court brought many refinements to the local gastronomy. Court chefs invented new desserts to tempt the royal fancy including *zabaglione* (whipped egg yolks and wine). Piedmont has more desserts, cakes and biscuits than any other region in Italy. The famous *gianduiotti* chocolates originate in Turin, using local hazelnuts, and even today the local shop windows display rarified assortments.

The centre of Turin seems full of antique shops, booksellers and cafés evoking the leisured past. At '*Baratti*', number 29 Piazza Castello, six or seven types of brioches are served in the morning and you can still sample Cavour and Alexandre Dumas' favourite breakfast drink – *bicerin* – made from coffee, hot chocolate and milk. At number 24 Piazza San Carlo, the elegant square built on the site of the Roman amphitheatre, the '*Caffe Torino*', serves formal afternoon tea, complete with silver teapots and Piedmontese *aperitivi* in the evening. Vermouth (*vermuttion*) was known in some form to the ancient Romans but was first made commercially in Turin in 1786. The name comes from the German *wermut* (wormwood). Martini Rosso's original formula was distilled by the herbalist 'Abello', which is still to be found stocking over 18,000 roots, leaves and flowers in Via Monte di Pietà, number 5.

Turin suffered morally and economically when it ceased to be the capital of Italy in 1864, but the development of the motor industry brought new prosperity, and today Fiat has made it one of Italy's leading industrial cities. The new industrial tempo has brought changes to the structure of the day and, consequently, to eating habits. Each citizen used to have his regular restaurant and bar which served as a sort of private club, where it was difficult to eat outside normal mealtimes – 12.30 lunch and 8 o'clock dinner. Today, there are bars like '*Augusto*' in Via Roma (number 86) which serves food all day, until 2 o'clock in the morning, and there are many gastronomic shops selling delicious, ready-prepared, take-away food. These shops fill the gaps left by vanishing home cooks and working wives, but they also provide the visitor with a lavish, multi-course picnic, or an interesting snack. The best of these include '*Gallo*' in Corso Sebastopoli (number 161), '*Baudracco*' in Corso V. Emanuele II (number 62) and '*Rosaschino*' in Via Pietro Micca (number 9).

In the hills around Turin a different culinary heritage exists which has grown up side by side with the court tradition. Piedmontese country cooking is hearty and robust, designed to ward off the cold and satisfy appetites sharpened by hard agricultural work. Perhaps it can best be appreciated in autumn when there is a nip in the air. The *nebbiola* grape, with its violet fragrance, father of the great Piedmontese red wines, gets its name from the *nebbia* (mist) which usually makes its first appearance around grape harvest time. The magnificent white truffles, costing a king's ransom, found around Alba, are in season from the middle of October to the end of December. It is worth planning a trip to this region then to try them, since they are at their best eaten on their home ground when they have been freshly found. They turn a simple dish of tagliolini (locally called *tajarin*), risotto or *fonduta* (melted cheese) into an unforgettable experience, and no preserved truffle can prepare you for their incredible perfume.

Because this is a great rice producing area, risotto is very common, and so are frogs, found in the flooded paddy fields and served as a local delicacy. Home-made pasta is usually cut into thin ribbons, *tajarin*, or used to make stuffed agnolotti. The great wines find their way into many of the meat courses and the local rabbit, hare, quail, partridge, pheasant and chamois are usually cooked in a Dolcetto sauce, or some other wine. When beef or veal are braised – *brasato al barolo* – the meat is traditionally marinated for 8 days before the slow cooking begins. Meats are often served with *polenta* made from yellow corn (maize) flour. In Piedmontese cooking nothing is wasted, and chicken crests, giblets and other parts of the intestines (*filoni*) are used to make interesting dishes, including *finanziera*, a dish so-called because it was popular with Turin bankers at the beginning of the century.

Villagers used to rely on communal bread ovens, so meat is not traditionally roasted. *Fritto misto* is very popular for celebrations, when many different meats, offal, vegetables and sweet semolina are dipped in batter and crisply fried. A great *fritto misto* may contain more than 15 different ingredients. The majestic *bollito misto*, served for great family gatherings, is made of boiled veal, beef, ham, tongue and sausage, and this is usually served with sharp sauces, *bagnetto verde* or *rosso*. The gravy from the *bollito* is served as a broth since soup is highly prized in this region. In the last century, the law stated that condemned prisoners should be given a bowl of soup before execution so that they finished life on a high note.

Before the first World War, homes were often isolated by winter snow and families learned to be self-sufficient. Stores of sugar, spices and salt were bought in and many one-course meals were invented using eggs, grains and dried vegetables. Anchovies were used to replace expensive salt. The famous *bagna cauda* made a tasty, filling dish in which edible thistles (*cardi*), were dipped in hot anchovy butter. The hills provide good grazing so the region enjoys a good supply of milk, butter and cheese. Traditionally butter is used in all recipes instead of olive oil and cheese plays a very important rôle on the menu. *Fonduta*, made from melted fontina cheese, is used with pasta, rice and meat, and in season it is often topped by delicious shavings of white truffle. Cheese is served after the meat course and includes fresh *robiola*, *bra*, and the rather pungent *brôss*, made from fresh cheese fermented with wine and *grappa*. Cream and eggs are the basis of many desserts including *biancomangiare*, *panna cotta* and the chocolate or coffee *bonèt*. Fresh peaches are stuffed with crumbled almond macaroons, and the local hazelnuts appear in many guises.

The red wines of this area were praised by Julius Caesar when he paused at La Morra, near Barolo, on his way to Gaul. They are served with great pride and usually decanted. The younger Dolcetto and Barbera wines usually appear early on in the meal, while Barolo or Barbaresco are served in beautiful, large glasses with the meat and cheese course. Traditionally the slightly fizzy Freisa is served with *bagna cauda*, Dolcetto with truffled dishes, Grignolino with *fritto misto* and Barbera with *bollito misto*.

In Piedmont, meals are served rather early so unless you are going to an ultra fashionable restaurant you should plan to lunch at around 12.30 and dine at 8 o'clock.

Del Cambio
Piazza Carignano 2, Turin
Tel. (011) 546690

Del Cambio first opened its doors in 1757 when the whole Piazza Carignano was rebuilt to match the baroque style of the new Teatro Carignano. It soon became the haunt of fashionable Turin and when, in 1848, the Palazzo Carignano, where Vittorio Emanuele II had been born, became the seat of Piedmont's Chamber of Deputies, the Members of Parliament made it their 'local'. Count Camille Cavour, the astute Turin-born politician who was the architect of the unification of Italy, became a 'regular' until his death in 1861. Today his table is marked by a discreet plaque with the national colours, and *Del Cambio* has become a gastronomic national monument. The atmosphere is hushed and elegant and formal waiters provide impeccable service. The wine list offers a great selection of the best Piedmont

wines and some great French wines.

There are three menus to choose from. The general *à la carte* menu includes specialities from Piedmont like *fritto misto* or *risotto al vino barolo*, plus dishes from other regions, like pasta with *pesto* or grilled sole from the Adriatic, and more international dishes such as rack of lamb or French onion soup. The well-balanced daily *à la carte* menu offers a good choice of new, light dishes like asparagus and scampi in a watercress sauce and dishes researched from old recipes such as the 1821 *carbonata vecchia Torino*. The third short, fixed-price set menu includes delights like marrow (squash) flowers stuffed with creamed truffles, and fresh pasta filled with mushrooms.

Del Cambio provides a perfect introduction to Turin and Piedmont's history, and the food and wine are worthy of its heritage. Booking is essential.

Price: *Expensive; Amex, Diners, Visa*
Closed: *Sundays and August*
Location: *Central Turin*

Balbo

Via Andrea Doria II, 10125 Turin
Tel. (011) 511743

Once upon a time this restaurant, conveniently located just a few mintues' walk from the elegant Piazza San Carlo, which is the bustling heart of Turin day and night, was a humble pizzeria. Today, the proprietor and chef, Luigi Caputo, is much more ambitious. He has created a small but quite formal establishment which offers not just the traditional regional food of Piedmont, but makes a considerable bow towards light, modern tastes.

The choice is between a fairly short *à la carte* menu, which will usually include such seasonable specialities as *risotto con tartufi d'Alba* (risotto with truffles), and two set menus. The moderately priced business menu proposes a modest four courses that may begin with *charlotte di melanzane, zucchini e peperoni* (vegetable mould) followed by *tagliatellini verdi con fiori di zucca e gamberetti* (pasta strings with marrow (squash) flowers and shrimps) and *piccione al miele con porri alla valdese* (pigeon with honey and leeks) and with a fruit bavarian cream for dessert.

But Luigi Caputo really prides himself on his six course gastronomic menu that can best be digested slowly over a long evening of conversation and good wine. It began, for me, with steamed sturgeon (*storione al vapore con insalatine all'aceto balsamino*) thence to *agnolotti monferrini al sugo arroso* and *filetto di pagello* (sea bream *al peperone rosso* – with red sweet peppers). The *pagello*, in particular, was fresh and flavourful. Then a strawberry sorbet before a great dish of *funghi porcini* with thin slices of potato, the whole flavoured with basil; a wonderful way to have a vegetarian main course and absolute confirmation that this autumn mushroom delicacy can stand on its own and does not need to be served with pasta or meat.

Then came a board with great wedges of local cheese, a course you do not find generally in Italy, but a regular feature in Piedmont, where many of the best cheeses are made. I was tempted by a Castelmagno, a hard white cheese, and Murianengo, a delicious regional cousin of gorgonzola. And finally a light fruit bavarian cream surrounded by a crimson lake of raspberry sauce.

The wine list at *Balbo* is strong on local Piedmont wines. I had a white Arneis with the fish and pasta; and a good red Nebbiola with the remainder of the meal. The list includes excellent Barolos from Alfredo Prunotto.

The service, at what has become one of Turin's more fashionable restaurants, is very professional and attentive; not somewhere where you have to beckon for the waiter.

Price: Expensive; Amex, Eurocard, Visa
Closed: Monday; July
Location: Central Turin, near Piazza San Carlo

San Giorgio
Borgo Medioevale al Valentino, Turin
Tel. (011) 6692131

The setting is like a fairy-tale as you arrive at this perfect, turreted castle on the banks of the river Po. For the Piedmont Great Exhibition of 1884, it was decided to reconstruct a medieval castle complete with its little village settlement. Today this great castle stands surrounded by little artisan houses in narrow alleys and, at its foot on the banks of the Po, we find *San Giorgio*.

The restaurant was opened in 1922 by the parents of the present owner, Signor Gallo, and since he was born on the premises, he was christened 'Giorgio'. The setting is enchanting with its riverside terrace left uncovered in warm weather. In the evening the atmosphere is formal with candle-lit tables and soft piano music. At around 10.00p.m. a singer begins a medley of nostalgic songs which are completely in tune with the atmosphere. There is no fear of her being tempted away to a rival establishment since she is Albertina, Giorgio Gallo's wife.

There is a very long menu made up of Piedmontese dishes, other Italian regions' specialities and international favourites. Over 20 choices are offered for the first course, including *Piedmontese agnolotti* and *risotto al barolo*. The even longer list of main courses, both meat and fish, include a typical *costoletta con fonduta* and medieval-style *tournedos*. Many diners opt for dishes which are flambéd at the table to increase the spectacular aspect of the evening. The wine list is good and the service is very attentive so this is a good place to go for a special night out.

Price: Expensive; Amex, Visa
Closed: Tuesday, Wednesday, lunch and August
Location: on river bank

Tre Colonne

Corso Rosselli 1, Turin
Tel. (011) 587029

This pleasant restaurant, not too far from the historic centre of Turin, has a large terrace where you can eat a peaceful meal in warm weather, and a bright, attractive dining-room with three columns, hence the name. The proprietor and chef, Renzo Zancanaro, works busily in his kitchen while his wife, Angela, is happy to help you choose the best daily fare from the very long menu. The cooking has something for every taste and includes Piedmontese specialities, and dishes from other regions.

All the usual antipasti are available and I have eaten a fine salad of *ovoli* (egg mushrooms) here which are so good but difficult to find on any menu. The first course offers many types of risotto including *risotto al Barolo, funghi porcini* and scampi. In season, Renzo makes a very delicate risotto using asparagus and artichokes. He offers spaghetti and rigatoni as well as a good selection of home-made pasta, including pappardelle with aubergines (eggplant) and green tagliolini with gorgonzola cheese sauce. During the late autumn truffle season, he serves tagliolini with truffles. For those who like stuffed pasta, there are usually one or two varieties.

For the main course, many kinds of meat are available, grilled or cooked in interesting sauces. During the game season, *Tre Colonne* offers hare, pheasant and the mountain chamois, when available. There is a choice of fresh-water and sea fish ,and on my last visit I enjoyed an excellent sea bass baked in salt, which preserves all the flavour. There is a tempting dessert trolley and, if you order fresh fruit, a veritable cornucopia is borne to the table.

Price: Moderate; Amex, Diners
Closed: Saturday lunch Monday; August
Location: Ten minute taxi from centre

Ostu Bacu
Corso Vercelli 226, Turin
Tel. (011) 264579

Ostu Bacu is a small restaurant in the outskirts of the city of Turin where people come to eat real Piedmontese home cooking and drink the local wines. Maria and Elzo live above and the atmosphere is very relaxed as they regard the restaurant as an extension of their home. In the evening you often find them sitting at table chatting to their regular customers, getting up to cook or serve and then returning to their place at the table. The only touch of formality comes from the presence of a sommelier – their son, Claudio.

At *Ostu Bacu* (which means Bacchus' trattoria) wine is taken very seriously. Elzo has a very careful selection and he is always pleased to discuss the pros and cons of various vineyards and bottlers. He also has a great selection of *grappa* which should only be tried by those not intending to drive. The restaurant started out as a *grigio e verde* (a 'grey and green'), a bar serving *grappa* and sandwiches to the local workers. Maria's mother began to develop the food, and after re-building, it re-opened as a trattoria. At lunch it often seems an extension of Fiat, as swarms of grey-suited businessmen fill up the tables.

There is a long series of Piedmontese antipasti to be followed by Maria's *tajarin* (tagliolini) or *agnolotti*, risotto or the very traditional tripe minestrone. For the main course you will find steak, rabbit, guinea fowl and a good *fritto misto*. This is a good place to eat *fritto misto* because they will good-naturedly leave out the usually obligatory *cervello* (brains) for squeamish clients, although frog and snail dishes are available for those in search of these Piedmontese delicacies. In autumn, *funghi porcini* make their presence felt and when the truffle season starts (October to December) Maria serves generous portions of mouth-watering goodness. In winter, you will find *bagna cauda*, and a sumptuous *bollito misto* is served every Wednesday. Elzo has Piedmontese cheeses like the famous *brôss*, and a fair selection of desserts including *panna cotta* and hazelnut tart.

Price: Inexpensive, Diners, Mastercard, Visa
Closed: Sunday and August
Location: Barriera di Milano area

Antica Zecca
Caselle Torinese, 10072 Turin
Tel. (011) 993733

Antica Zecca (The Old Mint), just across the road from Turin airport, is an elegant sixteenth century building that has been renovated to produce good food rather than gold and silver coin. Many Turin businessmen find its large, beamed dining room, with a great open brick grill at one end, ideal for welcoming foreign clients to Italy as they step off the plane. The trick, if you want to impress someone, is to reserve one of the two tables tucked into a corner close to the blazing hearth, where the chef, Bruno Libralon, prepares *spiedino di crostacei alla griglia* (shellfish on skewers) or *rognoncino di vitello grigliato nel suo grasso e valeriana* (veal kidneys grilled in their own juices with herbs). Libralon is a great ambassador of Italian cooking: he has travelled to Stockholm, New York and Tokyo to display his skills at special festivals. At home in Turin, however, he offers much more than grills. The choice of antipasti includes *pesce spada affumicato e melanzane grigliata* (cold, smoked swordfish with grilled aubergines/ eggplant) and *gratin di capesante e zucchini ai pistilli di zafferano* (hot scallops cooked in the oven with a little grated cheese, courgettes/ zucchini and a sauce of saffron). For the pasta course you may be offered *tagliatelle al ragù di funghi porchini* (tagliatele with ceps) or *risotto, code di scampi e fiori di zucca* (with scampi and marrow (squash) flowers).

The desserts are also a serious proposition – perhaps the delicate *bavarese alle fragole di bosco* (bavarian cream with wild strawberries) or, more spectacular, *crêpe milligusti* or *pesche margherita*, both of which are flamed at your table. The wine list embraces a broad choice of moderately priced local wines, such as white Arneis de Piemonte and red Barbera d'Alba Piani Romualdo di Monforte from Alfredo Prunotto, together with the more expensive '*i grandi rossi del Piemonte*' including some excellent 1982 Barbarescos and 1974 and 1982 Barolos.

The restaurant itself takes up one wing of the old Mint; the rest of the building is a hotel (Jet Hotel). Together they make a pleasant exception to the usual run of food or accommodation at an international airport.

Price: Expensive, Amex, Mastercard, Diners, Visa
Closed: Monday and first two weeks in August
Location: 14 kms from city centre, opposite airport

Langhe

*I*n the heart of Piedmont, between Asti and Cuneo, lies the hilly region known as the 'Langhe', famous for its noble red wines, opulent white truffles, rich *funghi porcini* and delicious cheeses. This is one of the most interesting regions of Italy with its small, wine-producing villages, romantic castles and towers, and warm, unstinting hospitality.

La Contea
Piazza Cocito, 8 Neive
Tel. (0173) 67126

La Contea is a relaxed, gastronomic haven created by Claudia and Tonino Verro. Tonino is a great wine expert, and Claudia loves to research old, forgotten regional recipes. When they were first married, Claudia found she had a full house for dinner every night since Tonino's exuberant hospitality knows no limits. A logical move was to start a restaurant and, in 1977, the year their daughter Elisa was born, Claudia and Tonino opened *La Contea*, in an old house in the centre of the town, which had once belonged to the Counts of Neive.

La Contea has an archaic, uncontrived charm due to the simplicity with which Claudia and Tonino have refurbished the house to meet their needs. The bar has been furnished with a massive antique wooden counter decorated with a beautifully carved and painted fruit design. The dining-rooms possess the grace of another era with their frescoed ceilings, elaborate wallpapers and wide, curved doors. Beautiful Riedel glasses shimmer on the tables and Tonino has one of the richest wine cellars in the area.

Claudia's menus are clearly displayed outside, three set menus to choose from and an *à la carte* selection. All are based on traditional dishes from Langhe in some cases lightened to suit modern tastes and designed to harmonise with the great local wines – Barbaresco, Dolcetto and Barolo. The menus are incredibly good value for money, and the *degustazione* selection allows you to try all the local specialities.

Tonino usually suggests you start with a white Arneis Castello di Neive and this goes very well with Claudia's warm weather version of *bagna cauda* served as a sauce on thin fillets of sweet yellow peppers. There are usually four or five little antipasti,

depending on the season, but Claudia nearly always includes *tartrà* – a sort of savoury egg custard made from onions, lots of fresh herbs and grated truffles.

Soup is highly prized in Piedmont, and Claudia prepares steaming bowls of fragrant broth using *funghi porcini*, truffles or fresh vegetables according to the time of year. The pasta selections are delectable and every day fresh *tajarin*, or tagliolini are prepared using 20 egg yolks to every kilo of flour.

The main course offers lamb, beef and veal with fresh herbs and good wine sauces and in winter months, hare, pheasant and other game when available. Claudia often serves duck cooked with Favorita wine and shoulder of veal cooked in Barbaresco. A good cheese board contains local cheeses and Claudia's home-made *brôss* made from *robiola* cheese fermented with *grappa* and white wine. There is a very good choice of desserts including a tart made from the local hazelnuts.

La Contea has a few rooms for overnight guests. In the morning, refreshed, you can start the day with a typical Piedmontese farm worker's breakfast consisting of fresh cheese and home-made *salame*, and indulge in the delicious home-made apricot and plum jams.

A visit to *La Contea* is an unusual experience not to be missed. It is also possible to buy the best local wines at *cantina* prices from Tonino, and Claudia sells jars of her fermented cheese and jams.

Price: Moderate set menus; Amex, Visa
Closed: Sunday evening, Tuesday. Usually open every day in truffle season (October to December)
Location: 31 km from Asti, 12 km NE Alba

~ RECIPE ~
Summer Bagna Cauda
Sweet Peppers with Anchovy Sauce from La Contea, Neive

4 cloves garlic and their weight in anchovy fillets,
when cleaned of oil or salt preserving solution
a small handful of fresh herbs including,
if possible, parsley, chives, marjoram, basil
60ml/4 tbsp olive oil
freshly ground black pepper
4 yellow sweet peppers

Liquidise all the ingredients except the sweet peppers and taste for seasoning: with the anchovies no more salt may be needed. Moisten the peppers with olive oil and grill (broil) for several minutes until it is possible to remove the skins. Remove the seeds and slice the soft peppers into small, elegant slivers. Divide into four portions and serve with the anchovy sauce poured over the top. Serves 4.

Ristorante Brezza
Via Lomondo 2, Barolo
Tel. (0173) 56191

In Barolo, the birthplace of the great red wine, the Brezza family runs a comfortable, modern restaurant. In good weather you can eat on the peaceful terrace facing the old castle while behind you the vineyards stretch away to the horizon. The Brezza family started their professional life here in 1885 as wine producers. They still produce and sell wine and even today some of the original casks are in use in the old cellars. Giovanna, grandmother to Oreste Brezza, one of the present owners, was a very good cook. Her grandson recalls her *mani d'oro* (golden hands), and the surprise midnight snacks she made for him, with great nostalgia and tenderness. She and her husband, Antonio, started to serve food in 1910 when the new railway linking Piedmont and Liguria had a fixed stop just in front of their wine *cantina*. During the First World War, in the men's absence, she ran everything with great competence and the family gradually expanded their activities. Today, they are wine producers, restaurateurs and hoteliers. Each of their modern, comfortable bedrooms is named after a *grand cru* wine and every room contains at least one piece of traditional Piedmontese furniture.

In the kitchen, tradition is strictly upheld. The antipasti consists of many little dishes, typically of this region, including some tasty little herb fritters. The pasta is fine home-made *tajarin*, or tagliolini, served with truffles from October to December, or *agnoletti al plin*, stuffed with a vegetable and meat mixture. The main courses include typical dishes like beef cooked slowly in Barolo wine, *faraona all'Arneis* (guinea fowl cooked in white Arneis wine), and rabbit stewed with savoury herbs.

There is a good choice of local cheeses – *bra*, *raschera*, *casatelmagno* and the famous *brôss* – *robiole* fermented with wine and *grappa*. These cheeses taste sublime with a last glass of a 1982 Barolo. The desserts are local specialities like hazelnut tart and *zabaglione* made with Barolo wine.

Price: *Moderate; credit cards not accepted*
Closed: *Tuesday; January*
Location: *42 km from Asti, 56 km from Cúneo*

Asti

*A*sti, home of the sparkling sweet 'Asti Spumante', and many good red wines, is such a thriving town that the medieval centre is rather overwhelmed by sprawling urban development. Yet Asti has a strong sense of tradition with an annual fair celebrating regional artisan crafts and gastronomic specialities.

Ristorante Gener Neuv

Lungotanaro 4, Asti
Tel. (0141) 57270

Gener Neuv, on the banks of the river Tanaro, is planted firmly in the Astigiano sense of tradition. When, in 1971, Piero and Pina Fassi decided to open a restaurant, they took over this historic place and gladly kept the name, only adding a *'neuv'* to indicate the change of ownership.

'*Pian, pian, pien, pien*' (slowly, slowly) has been taken to heart, and eating here is a leisurely affair. The service is smoothly professional in the dining-room with its huge open fireplace, yet Piero makes every guest feel genuinely welcome and the restaurant remains very much a family affair.

A good *aperitivo* is a glass of Arneis, and a typical meal starts with a series of light, unusual antipasti. At some point, it is time to move on to the young red wine, and I remember a wonderful 1987 Bruno Giacosa Docetto d'Alba blessing a small gruyere cheese tart and delectable *funghi porcini* cooked in vine leaves. Among the many good first courses, I love the delicate fresh pasta and bean soup. For the main course in Piedmont it is usual to move on to an older, full red wine such as a Barbaresco or Barolo. The Prunotto Barolo 1982 is splendid and goes very well with saddle of rabbit, lamb or veal cooked in Barolo, or the great Piedmontese speciality, *finanziera*. From October to December, the famous white truffles are in season and they play a dominant role in the winter menu. There is a good choice of desserts and home-made pastries but in Asti it seems fitting to end the meal with a light *zabaglione al Moscato* (whisked egg and wine).

Price: Moderate to expensive; Amex, Diners, Visa
Closed: Sunday evening, Monday
Location: on the river Tanaro, on S456 direction Alba

Ristorante Guido
Piazza Umberto 1, 27 Costigliole D'Asti
Tel. (0141) 966012

Guido is one of the few restaurants lauded throughout the whole of Italy. Italians from all regions make pilgrimages to Costigliole D'Asti to visit this national treasure. At first sight, the setting is a little disappointing since the piazza is very ordinary and the restaurant is in a semi-basement. Once inside, however, one's mood swiftly changes.

This stylish restaurant is run by the Alciati family who do all the work themselves. Guido and Lidia started in 1958, with Guido travelling tirelessly around the region searching out the best *materia prima* for Lidia to transform into regional specialities and imaginative new dishes. Their sons, now grown up, provide first-class professional back-up.

Every evening (*Guido's* is open only in the evening) the menu changes according to the season and the best produce available. I remember a light *zucchine* mousse with shavings of white truffles in a swirling green and yellow sauce, and a wonderfully light salad of turkey breast marinated in lemon. In the autumn and winter, you might find soups made with *funghi porcini* or truffles and small *agnolotti* dressed with fresh sage and melted butter. The main course is based on meat (which Guido selects at the cattle market before the animal has been butchered), free-range poultry, game in season and river fish .It is pointless to be too specific about individual dishes because Lidia invents an endless repertoire with innumerable variations on a theme. Regular customers sometimes phone days in advance to request a favourite dish although Guido usually keeps a note of what he prepares for his guests so that they do not repeat the same dishes. However, there is always a wide choice and most go to Guido's as a gastronomic adventure and they want to be surprised.

Now to the wines. This is a restaurant for the wine lover: a veritable Aladdin's Cave of wine. And not just the splendid local

Arneis or Barolos. You can take your choice of the best of Robert Mondavi from California, a Corton-Charlemagne from Burgundy or a Château d'Yquem from Bordeaux. The home-grown Barolos date from 1958, the year Guido started his restaurant (though he hastens to tell you the wine was aged in the cask for three years before it was bottled). Guido's cellar holds 50,000 bottles, but he only started a wine list a few years ago, preferring to advise his guests of the best wine to go with their food. Booking is essential.

Price: Expensive; Amex
Closed: Sunday; July and August; midday
Location: 15 kms S. of Asti, off S456

La Fioraia
Via Marconi 2, Castello D'Annone
Tel. (0141) 60106
(some time in 1989 the restaurant is moving 200 metres into the hills to Via Tagliate, 26. Same tel. no.)

This small elegant restaurant, run by Ornella and Mario Cornero, with the help of their daughter Manuela, offers delightfully light, imaginative cooking. The menu which changes according to season is chiefly influenced by Piedmontese culinary traditions, but the style of cooking is highly individual and offers some pleasant surprises. I discovered *La Fioraia* by chance one hot, dusty Sunday in June and I could not believe my luck as I sat down in the cool, peaceful dining room with a chilled bottle of Arneis to enjoy a salmon (sea) trout mousse with basil sauce, and sweet pepper fillets served with a creamy tuna fish filling. This was followed by a slice of honeycomb-textured basil omelette, stuffed and rolled to give a spiralled effect. Instead of pasta, I had a fresh asparagus risotto and, for the main course, boned leg of lamb wrapped in crisp pastry and served with a mushroom sauce. I finished the meal with an unforgettable melon mousse.

When I returned a few years later in autumn the local *funghi porcini* and truffles were in season, adding a new dimension to this splendid cooking. Mario has a good choice of regional wines and this is a good place to drink the local Grignolino.

Price: Moderate, credit cards not accepted
Closed: Monday; August
Location: 11kms from Asti, on the road to Alessandria

Giardino Da Felicin
Via D. Vallada 18, Monforte D'Alba
Tel. (0173) 78225

This country restaurant was started by the present owner's father, Felicin, hence the name 'Felicin's Garden'. The restaurant is set just off the main square of this wine-producing village and the terrace has a superb view across the vineyarded hills to the Alps. Felicin served with the army in Libya in 1922 and started to cook in order to eat Italian, not Arabic, food. His son, Giorgio, is a splendid host. He emerges from his kitchen from time to time to suggest, in perfect English, various specialities from the menu. Rosina, his wife, is a graceful châtelaine moving from table to table to make sure everything runs smoothly.

In warm weather the meal usually starts with a glass or two of very light white Favorita, and a series of delightful antipasti. The guinea fowl pâté studded with truffles and walnuts is very good and I shall long remember a little dish of *funghi porcini* cooked in a mushroom cream sauce. A young Dolcetto or Barbera wine is usually served at this point, with the Barolo and Barbaresco being reserved for the main course and cheese. However, if you have not booked one of the upstairs bedrooms, it is probably better to settle for one or the other but not both. I enjoyed a Renato Ritti La Morra Barolo with my pasta course and stayed with it to the end of the meal. I ate home-made tagliolini with *funghi porcini*, but in the truffle season, from October to December, Giorgio serves truffles with these *tajarin*, and with stuffed pasta, *ravioli col plin tartufati*. One of his great specialities is *topinambur* (Jerusalem artichokes) tossed with butter and truffles. The main courses include various meats cooked in the local wines and game in season. There is a very good cheese trolley and, if you still have some red wine in your glass, do try some of the local toma d'Alba Cappello. The desserts are as good as the rest of the meal and, to avoid an anguished choice, there is a mixed plate containing various tiny portions.

Giorgio and Rosina have several comfortable bedrooms furnished with some lovely old Piedmontese pieces of furniture. If you want to do full justice to the food and wines plan an overnight stay.

Price: Moderate; Visa
Closed: Wednesday; January and February
Location: 15 km SW of Alba

VENICE
& the Veneto

*V*enice, built on water, shimmers with distorted images. The reflections are endless in this city which invented the art of making mirrors and was prepared to kill to defend its monopoly of this frivolity. Every visitor through the ages has viewed Venice through a different lens ranging from D.H. Lawrence's 'abhorrent, green, slippery city' to Goethe's description of the Grand Canal as 'the most beautiful street in the world'.

However, there seems to be some feeling today of disenchantment and two widely differing sources agree that Venice has become too commercial. A leading British newspaper writes: 'La Serenissima is now Rip-off City'. The Italian *Accademia della Cucina*, in a restaurant guide written for Italians, says: 'today, in Venice, it is possible to eat very well but it is a rare privilege and more often one eats in an inconsistent, irritating way and it is frequently absurdly expensive.'

The visitor to Venice needs to retain a sense of perspective and choose warily. Venice has always been a commercial city with an eye for the main chance, supplying what was in demand, be it shipping, spices, jewels or courtesans. Today, Venice still tries to sell people what they want and the fall in gastronomic standards is in many cases caused by tourists who have no interest in Venetian culinary traditions. The glorious Venetian risotto is difficult, it needs to be prepared freshly for each customer, and inevitably it takes 20 minutes at least to cook. If the customer is just as happy with a comparatively quick plate of pasta a restaurateur can feel 'why not?'. Previously good places can go downhill quite quickly. There are also some cases of downright dishonesty. Some fashionable restaurants go so far as to employ a two-priced menu – one for Venetians and one for foreign visitors. The foreigners pay dearly for the pleasure of dining side by side with Venetians whom they are indirectly subsidising.

Happily it is still possible to eat well in some restaurants and traditional Venetian cooking is very varied with many interwoven strands. Plain, elementary fish cooking dates from the earliest times when Vandals forced the Venetians to flee to the Lagoon and vegetables were then cultivated on the islands. During the Dark Ages, Venice traded with the east and shortly after the Holy Roman Empire was established little bags of imported spices known as *sacchettis Venetis* were sold for vast sums of money. A bishop from Castello left pepper, saffron, cinnamon, cumin and coriander as a valuable inheritance in his will.

Until the fourteenth century, Venice looked to the Arab world for culinary refinement, but Venice then established herself as a sophisticated city with an opulent style. Several Venetian-inspired books about food were published and Venice enjoyed a trade monopoly in spices, salt, pepper, sugar and coffee. Sugar from Arabia, used first as a medicine, was sold on the Rialto grain by grain because it was so expensive, and was used to bribe or reward business contacts. In 1585, a Venetian diplomat in Constantinople wrote home about a boiling black liquid and by 1640 in Venice, 15 years before the rest of Europe, coffee was sold for medicinal purposes. Once it was found to be quite palatable with sugar, the first coffee shop soon opened in St. Mark's Square. The famous St. Mark's Square cafés which still exist today, *Quadri* and *Florian*, were established in the eighteenth century and when Venice came under Austrian rule, Austrians frequented *Quadri* while the Venetians tended to congregate at *Florian*. The Venetian playwright, Goldoni, writing in the eighteenth century spends a lot of time discussing food, and in his plays he gives recipes for sardines in *saor* sauce, *fritto misto*, fried cream dessert and a good cup of coffee. Napoleon abolished the ghetto before he sold Venice to the Austrians and many Jewish specialities were absorbed into Venetian cooking, including many *melanzane* (aubergine or eggplant) dishes, the home-made pasta *bigoli*, the pasta pie *frinsinsal* and various dishes using duck and geese.

Modern Venetian cooking is simple and rich at the same

time. The textures are usually smooth and creamy and the tastes are subtle and delicate avoiding robust flavours. Rice, which grows throughout the valley of the Po, plays a very important part in the diet. The Venetians, being a sea-faring people, like their risotto semi-liquid *'all'onda'* (like a wave) – if you move the plate the risotto ripples like a wave – and this risotto is made with whatever vegetable, fish or meat comes to hand. The most common use young peas in *risi e bisi*, or *nero di seppie* (squid), or small shrimps from the Lagoon. Polenta made with maize (*granturco*) is cooked in many ways; and the yellow polenta is usually served with meat while the white maize from Friuli is used to make the more delicate polenta to accompany fish. Pasta is not a traditional dish in the Veneto region except for *pasta e fagioli* and the rustic *bigoli* usually served with meat sauce.

Various Venetian soups are made from fish and shellfish but these do not have the addition of saffron or chilli pepper like famous Mediterranean fish soups. *Broeto* has a velvety texture with all the fish bones removed before serving. A thick meat soup, almost a stew, *sopa coada* is made from boned pigeons and traditionally it is cooked in an earthenware pot. *Polenta e oscei* (a speciality from Vicenza) is made with any small birds available. Poultry is very popular and there are many dishes using duck, guinea fowl, capons, geese and turkey, which is delicious cooked with pomegranates. *Baccalà* (salt fish) was introduced by sailors returning from the northern seas. What they really brought back was dried cod (*stoccafisso*) but it was mistakenly given the name for salt cod and the name has stuck. This dried cod, although it sounds unprepossessing, is made into a delicious cream *baccalà mantecato*.

Probably the most widely known of all Venetian dishes is calves' liver cooked with onions which Venetians claim as their invention. *Fegato alla veneziana* is eaten throughout Italy.

Fish, humble and rare, dominates Venetian cooking, coming from the Adriatic, the Lagoon, the rivers and lakes. The fish is roasted, grilled (or broiled), fried, stuffed or preserved. Sardines or small sole are served in *saor*, a sauce made from fried onions, vinegar, spices, pine nuts and

sultanas (golden raisins), which was traditionally a way of preserving fish so that it could be eaten for several days.

The French writer, Georges Sand wrote that gluttony was the Venetian deadly sin, and Venetians certainly find many excuses even today to eat and drink. Biscuits, cakes and cookies are great Venetian delicacies and there is a wide selection. *Rosa Salva* in San Salvador is an old establishment where a great assortment can be sampled on the spot or taken away. There are a great number of wine shops scattered throughout the city and they do a brisk trade from 9 or 10.0 a.m. Instead of elevenses or mid-morning coffee breaks, employees leave their offices to fill *il vuoto delle 11.0* (the eleven o'clock gap) with a glass of wine. There are often over a hundred opened bottles to choose from, and a tasty snack that resembles cocktail party fare. Wine shops are usually open until 1.30 p.m. and then they re-open from 4.0 p.m. until 9.0 p.m. or later. Visitors will find that they make a very attractive alternative to the self-service fast food bars catering for tourists. They are also much cheaper. Little glasses of wine or spirits are known in Venice as *ombre* (shadows), and often two elegant ladies will enjoy an *ombre* with a *cicheto* (a nibble) together.

WINE BARS:

At the *Enoteca Al Volto* (Cala Cavalli S. Luca Tel: (041) 5228945) the great wine list consists of seven pages each of Tuscan and Piedmont wines, four pages of Veneto wines and five pages of Friuli. Ten pages of French wines are also included. You can enjoy a glass of wine and a delicious snack for less than the price of tea or coffee at a fashionable café. Open sandwiches with smoked salmon and mozzarella cheese are typical quick dishes on offer. There are seats for about twenty and room to stand at the bar. Open: 9.0 a.m. – 1.30 p.m.; 4.0 p.m. – 9.0 p.m.

Also good is the *Osteria Terà Assassini* (Rio d'Assassini Tel: (041) 5287986). A very good selection of wines, simple snacks and hot meals is available here. Each day features a speciality: Tuesday and Friday – fish, with *baccalà* on Friday as well; Thursday – *bollito misto*; Wednesday – *pasta e fagioli*. The interior is very attractive with beamed ceilings, old photos of Venice and lamps decorated with hand-made Burano lace. The clientele are mainly artists and musicians. Open 10.0 a.m. – 4.0 p.m. and 6.0 p.m. – 11.0 p.m.

Do Forni
Calle Specchieri, Venice
Tel: (041) 5232148

Eligio Paties is a great professional restaurateur and *Do Forni* (the name means 'two ovens') contrives to please everyone. The long, narrow foyer seating 30 is modelled on the luxurious 'Orient Express' dining-car and the atmosphere is one of muted elegance. The large main room, swathed in orange material like an eastern tent, is more relaxed and even at the height of the season the good-humoured waiters have time to joke and chat with the customers. Twenty-two waiters ensure very good service and the kitchens can be relied on to produce well-prepared, authentic dishes even when under considerable pressure. In the summer, when the city can wilt beneath the tourist invasion, and standards slip considerably in many places, *Do Forni* restored my faith in Venetian restaurants.

The very long menu is designed to offer something for everyone and there are many meat and vegetable dishes for those who do not like fish. At the beginning of the meal the diner gets a good selection of breads and the house *aperitivo* while he mulls over the choice. From the well-chosen wine list, I usually order a Friuli Sauvignon which goes well with fish. The antipasti contains the usual good shrimps, spider crab and other shellfish but there is also a deliciously tasty creamed salt cod *baccalà mantecato* served on polenta and a tender *polipo affogato*, literally 'drowned' or stewed octopus. There is a good selection of pasta dishes but the risottos are incredibly good, made with what is best from the daily catch. There is a nourishing fish soup from Chioggia which should be tried, but I find it hard to choose between fillets of *rombo* (halibut) cooked with black olives and sea bass served on a bed of potatoes flavoured with rosemary. A simple salad of *rucola* (rocket or arugula) goes well with these fish dishes.

An exotic choice of desserts includes a lush soufflé which is served with a glass of *ramandolo* – the sweet wine from Friuli.

Price: *Moderate to expensive; all major credit cards*
Closed: *Thursday; part of November, December*
Location: *Water bus to San Marco stop*

Antico Martini

Campo San Fantin, Venice
Tel: (041) 5224121

Antico Martini is an elegant restaurant in the centre where you can be sure of good food and courteous service even at the height of the season. Emilio Baldi runs his restaurant with calm professionalism and the menu offers traditional Venetian dishes as well as other regional and international specialities.

The building has a long history with a restaurant established as Caffè San Fantin in the early eighteenth century. When the Fenice theatre was opened next door in 1792 the Caffè became the meeting place for patrons and artists alike and this tradition has continued. The restaurant has had its highs and its lows over the years as it has changed hands from time to time. The Baldi family took over in 1921 rather by accident. Emilio Baldi's father, originally from Tuscany, moved to Venice to market Tuscan wine. When the *Martini* was unable to pay its wine bill, Signor Baldi found himself the rather perplexed owner of this ailing, historic restaurant, and since he had no thought of changing career, he reorganised it to sell and recoup his losses. Instead he became 'hooked' and today his grandson, Antonio, is preparing to enter what has now become the family business.

Two comfortable dining-rooms and a courtyard in Campo San Fantin, glassed in during the cooler months, make up the restaurant today. There is a large *à la carte* menu, a gastronomic menu which offers good value but allows no choice, and a daily menu which changes according to the market produce available. An unusual smoked goose breast served with *rucola* (rocket or arugula) is among the antipasti, as well as the more usual luxury items. This is a very good place to order Venetian risotto, often made with tiny shrimps from the Lagoon or cooked with squid and their ink sacs to form a glistening black feast.

Martini Scala next door is the piano bar open from 10.0 p.m. until 3.30 a.m. where it is possible to dine with a shortened version of the *Antico Martini* menu. Their wine bar *Vino Vino* is open non-stop from 10.0 a.m. and serves a very good selection of wine by the glass or bottle.

Price: *Expensive; all major credit cards*
Closed: *Tuesday, Wednesday lunch; January, February, except for Carnival*
Location: *Water bus to S. Marco or S. Maria del Giglio*

La Corte Sconta
Calle del Pestrin, Venice
Tel: (041) 5227024

One of the best meals I have ever eaten in Venice was at this family-run trattoria tucked away between lovely old squares frequented almost exclusively by the local cats taking the sun. 'La Corte Sconta' means the hidden courtyard and two-thirds of the available tables are arranged in the rustic courtyard at the back of the dining-room. The restaurant used to be a *bottiglieria* or wine shop, and the local old men still come between meals to sit over a glass of wine playing cards. The décor remains very simple with paper place settings and communal tables.

The chef and proprietor, Claudio Proietto, worked as a land surveyor for the local council for 11 years before opening this restaurant where, with a love of cooking inherited from his grandfather, he prepares traditional local food with imaginative innovations. The city of Venice has lost a surveyor but gained an invaluable asset with *La Corte Sconta* which gives visitors good local food and genuinely friendly, pleasant service at a very honest price. Although word has spread, the trattoria remains unpretentious and unspoiled, and over a relaxed, leisurely meal you catch a glimpse of the Venice of the Venetians, that gives a genuine feeling of what Venice is all about.

The smiling Lucia explains the daily menu and you can safely follow her sage advice, which may lead you to simply-prepared scallops, mixed shellfish salad and dressed crab served in its shell.

The mussels are particularly good since they are stuffed with a sharp, light filling instead of the more usual, rather cloying cheese mixture. This is a good place to try the traditional sardines in *saor*, 'cooked' in a sauce of vinegar, nuts and sultanas (golden raisins), and the black risotto made with squid and their ink is not to be missed if it is on the menu. The main course offers well-prepared local fish and Claudio's special San Pietro fillets inspired by his travels in Thailand where he was intrigued by the interesting combination of seafood and fresh ginger. This is one of my favourite fish dishes with its sharp, clean taste. To finish your meal you can try the traditional local biscuits (cookies) served with a glass of *zabaglione*.

Price: Inexpensive; Amex, Visa, Mastercard
Closed: Sundays, Mondays; part of August
Location: By water bus to Arsenale stop

Gritti Palace
Campo Santa Maria del Giglio, Venice
Tel: (041) 5226044

The ultimate meal with a view, if you are feeling extravagant, is at the Gritti Palace. As Somerset Maugham wrote: 'there are few things in life more pleasant than to sit on the terrace of the Gritti when the sun about to set bathes in lovely colours the Salute which almost faces you.' The Gritti Palace, once the home of the 77th Doge, Andrea Gritti, was built in the fifteenth century, and it enjoys a superb location on the Grand Canal, its charm intact, and its clientele individual travellers. The restaurant offers a judicious selection of Venetian, Italian and international dishes with the addition of the chef's specialities. On the antipasti list, *prosciutto e melone* takes its place beside the Venetian *sfogi in saor* (small soles in a sweet-sour sauce), Molossol caviare, and *Bresaola Gritti Palace*, thin slivers of smoked beef served with grapefruit and *rucola* (rocket or arugula). Gazpacho soup appears with the *pasta e fagioli alla veneta*, and there are pasta dishes from Liguria and Sicily as well as the chef's special *taglierini verdi gratinati al prosciutto*.

A good wine list represents most Italian regions, and a small selection of wines from France, Austria, Germany and Spain.

Price: Very expensive; all major credit cards
Closed: Always open
Location: On the Grand Canal, near the S. Maria del Giglio water bus stop

Capitan Uncino
Camp S. Giacomo dell'Orio, Venice
Tel: (041) 721901

Camp S. Giacomo dell'Orio is one of the most beautiful squares in Venice with its lovely trees and an interesting ninth-century church which has an unusual wooden ceiling shaped in the form of a ship's keel. The square is off the main tourist track and the trattoria's clientele is largely local.

This small trattoria was taken over in 1983 by two brothers, Maurizio and Michele Rossato, who had grown up in a similar family restaurant. In warm weather, tables are set outside in the piazza and there is a reasonable menu which changes every day according to the best selection on the market. The cooking is traditionally Venetian with dishes like *baccalà mantecato* and *fegato alla veneziana*, but each day there are some other regional specialities to please the 'regulars'. There is a pleasant house wine and a small selection of other wines. Altogether, this is a friendly trattoria offering very good value for money.

Price: *Very inexpensive; credit cards not accepted*
Closed: *Tuesdays; November*
Location: *Water bus to S. Stae stop*

Da Ivo
Romo dei Fuseri, Venice
Tel: (041) 5205889

This small welcoming restaurant on a narrow street beside a canal (impossible to eat outside) is owned by Ivo Natali who originally came from Tuscany where his family has long been involved in restaurants. Here you will find the best of both the Venetian and Tuscan culinary traditions.

The mainly seafood antipasti includes *granseola* (spider crabs), scallops and *cappe saltate*, shellfish tossed in white wine, lemon, garlic and parsley. I have enjoyed an excellent pasta, *penne paesana*, made with *melanzane* (aubergine or eggplant), sweet peppers and olives and the black *risotto de seppie* (with squid) is equally good. For the main course, I recommend grilled *funghi porcini* when they are available, and there is always a good selection of meat.

Price: *Moderate to expensive; all major credit cards*
Closed: *Sunday; January*
Location: *Water bus to San Marco*

Antica Trattoria Ae Poste Vecie

Mercato Del Pesce, Rialto, Venice
Tel: (041) 721822

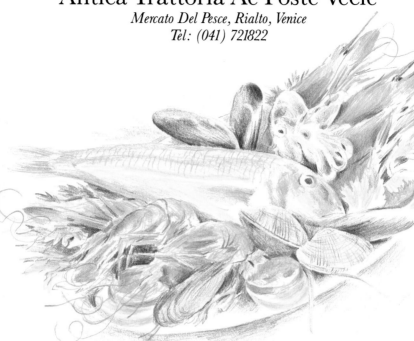

This attractive old trattoria, tucked away behind the Rialto fish market, used to be the post office and meeting place for the local merchants who met to discuss the state of the market and cargoes, due and overdue. Inevitably, this recalls Shakespeare's 'What news on the Rialto?', and Venetian tradition has it that Shylock himself, hearing he had made a handsome profit, here offered glasses of *slibowitz* to the host and postal clerk. The trattoria still boasts several venerable bottles of this fiery liqueur. After many changes this building was taken over recently by Dino Boscarato, owner of the well-known '*Amelia*' restaurant in industrial Mestre, who has saved what still remained. The inner dining-rooms boast huge old fireplaces which are lit in cold weather, and an unusual frieze of portraits painted at the turn of the century by an artist and customer, using 'regulars' as models. In the warmer months meals are served in the small terracotta courtyard and the diner is offered a *bellini* (champagne and peach juice) as an *aperitivo* while he studies the small but well-composed menu.

Given the location, fish obviously predominates, although there are meat dishes available. I have enjoyed delicious grilled scallops as an antipasto as well as a very good fish soup. Shellfish pasta dishes abound, Venetian *pasta e fagioli*, fettuccine with fresh tomatoes and basil, and authentic risottos. For the main course there is a good selection of grilled fish and shellfish and usually, depending on the market, *coda di rospo* (monkfish) cooked in black butter and capers, and fillets of sea bass with fresh tomato and basil. For those who prefer meat there is *fegato alla veneziana* or *carpaccio* (thinly sliced raw beef).

Price: *Moderate; Amex, Diners, Visa*
Closed: *Tuesdays; July, August*
Location: *Water bus to Rialto stop*

Osteria Da Fiore

Calle del Scaleter, San Polo, Venice
Tel: (041) 721308

Da Fiore is frequented almost exclusively by Venetians. The restaurant is small, elegant and comfortable with air-conditioning in the warmer months, but there is no outside terrace or beautiful view. Here the attraction is the marvellous fresh fish, beautifully cooked and combined in an imaginative way with fresh vegetables and wild herbs.

The restaurant started life many years ago as a *bottiglieria,* or wine shop, owned by Fiore and the entrance still has the traditional wine shop dispensing counter and relaxed, welcoming atmosphere. *Da Fiore* is now owned by Mara Zanetti and Maurizio Martin and they have built up a solid reputation with their short menu based on the best quality fish available. The antipasti is in the best lagoon tradition and consists of every kind of shellfish, rare or humble, cooked simply to bring out the flavour. There are several interesting pasta dishes like fettuccine with scampi and wild herbs, and I remember a perfect risotto made with scampi and *funghi porcini.* On another occasion, I enjoyed fillets of sea bass cooked with radicchio and I recall with pleasure young asparagus combined with delicate small fish. White polenta, a local speciality with a subtle taste, is served as an accompaniment. A few good desserts include *amaretti* (little almond biscuits or cookies) with *mascarpone* (cream cheese), fruit tart and light bavarian cream with fresh fruit.

Although there is a good wine list, I usually order the sparkling white house wine which is extremely pleasant and goes very well with the food.

Price: *Moderate; Amex, Diners, Visa*
Closed: *Sunday, Monday, Christmas, part of August*
Location: *Water bus to S. Tomà stop*

The Islands of the Lagoon

*A*way from central Venice, the islands of the Lagoon present a chance for peaceful escape, dazzling views and a number of restaurants offering good food, all of them pleasant and one or two memorable.

Mazzorbo

A pleasant trattoria, frequented mainly by local people, can be found on the island of Mazzorbo, reached by waterbus from Venice itself or by taking the wooden bridge from the island of Burano.

Antica Trattoria all Maddalena
Mazzorbo
Tel. (041) 730151

In the early 1900s this trattoria was founded by a local woman and her two daughters to cook fish and game found in the surrounding marshes for the boatmen who carried cargoes through the Lagoon in their *burchi* – large flat-bottomed boats.

In 1954 the Simoncin family bought the trattoria and the 'secret' recipe for the *Maddalena's* speciality, fettuccine in a wild duck sauce. Wild duck is at its best from September to April and during this period duck and polenta are also served as a main course. This trattoria offers many typical Venetian fish dishes including a very light *frittura mista*. The Maddalena still doubles as the local bar, serving drinks and snacks at most hours. At around 10 in the morning you can see a table full of local fishermen fortifying themselves with a nourishing *zuppa alla trippa parmigiana* (tripe soup), after arduous hours of fishing.

Price: *Inexpensive; credit cards not accepted*
Closed: *Thursday*
Location: *Waterbus 12 to Mazzorbo from the Fondamenta Nuove stop, Venice*

Murano

This picturesque centre of centuries of Venetian glass making is a ten-minute journey by waterbus from the Fondamenta Nuova stop in Venice. A very attractive little trattoria in its midst boasts the advantage of a terrace on the canal, *Ai Frati* (tel. 041 736694). The trattoria was founded in 1860. and is now run by the fifth generation of the Camozza family. This moderately priced trattoria is closed on Thursday and does not accept credit cards.

Burano

A small fishing village in the Lagoon, Burano is a 40-minute journey by waterbus from Venice Fondamenta Nuova stop. There are two small trattorias that repay a visit. *Ai Pescatori*, (tel. 041 730650) is a family run restaurant founded in 1880, with tables set out in a pleasant garden. This moderately priced trattoria is closed on Monday, and credit cards are not accepted.

Also on Burano is *Da Romano* (tel. 041 730030) which was established in the 1930s and is now run by Romano's son, Orazio. This relaxed trattoria is moderately priced, and closed on Tuesday. Credit cards are not accepted.

Torcello

Torcello was once an important town, believed to have been founded by Venetians fleeing Attila and his barbaric hordes. The seventh-century cathedral with its interesting mosaic of the Last Judgement suggests past glories.

Locanda Cipriani
Tel: (041) 730150

Among food lovers, Torcello is best known for the *Locanda Cipriani*, founded in 1938 by Guiseppe Cipriani who fell in love with the peaceful island. The Locanda has remained the same simple inn (only four bedrooms) that Ernest Hemingway loved so much; his friend, Guiseppe, kept it open during the winter of 1948 so that Hemingway could shoot the local wild duck and finish writing 'Across the River and into the Trees'.

Today the Locanda is managed by Bonifacio Brass, Guiseppe's young grandson while Dario De Zorzi runs the restaurant. A lovely cool terrace is the setting for lunch, served to visitors who can arrive from Venice by a special boat that leaves San Marco at the Danieli Hotel at 12.30. In the evening, when most of the visitors have departed, the island takes on a gentler mood and the *Locanda* serves quiet dinners to the few lucky residents and those arriving by privately arranged transport.

Price: *Expensive; all major credit cards*
Closed: *Tuesdays; November to mid-March*
Location: *Waterbus 12 to Torcello from Fundamenta Nuove stop, Venice*

Mira

*B*etween Venice and Padua the Brenta canal is studded with beautiful Palladian villas, and in the eighteenth century the elegant *burchiello*, a local flat-bottomed boat, carried illustrious passengers along the waterway. Today, there is a modern tourist boat making the same journey but a car or taxi leaves you free to explore at leisure and lunch out at a restaurant of your choice.

Trattoria Nalin
Via Novissimo, Mira
Tel: (041) 420083

A visit to Mira can enable you to see the Palazzo Foscarini which pleased both Thomas More and Byron and at the same time you can lunch at *Nalin*. This elegant fish restaurant facing the canal was opened in 1914 by Ernesto Nalin, grandfather of the present owner, Sergio.

There is always a good selection of shellfish for antipasto: I enjoyed delicious simply-cooked scallops which were followed by a faultless risotto. There is a good selection of pasta dishes, and this is a good place to try fish soup. The main course depends on the fish in the market but there is always a very light *fritto misto* and a good plate of mixed grilled fish. Most of the vegetables are home-grown and are served very simply so that the good natural flavour is not hidden. The dessert trolley is very tempting and the traditional *torta della nonna* is warmly recommended. I like both the house wines, a sparkling *prosecco* and a dry Tocai.

Price: Moderate; Amex, Diners, Visa
Closed: Sunday, Monday; August
Location: 21 km from Venice, water bus to Mestre then taxi

Verona

*V*erona, on the river Adige, with its impressive sixteenth-century walls, hosts an international opera and drama festival every summer in its large Roman arena with its perfect acoustics. Two important families, the Scaligere and the

Visconti, held power in turn until Verona came under Venetian domination which lasted for four centuries, a decisive influence on Verona's cooking.

Ristorante 'Arche'
Via Arche Scaligere 6, Verona
Tel: (045) 8007415

Every historic angle in Verona seems to be linked in some way to the tragic love of Romeo Montecchi, Guelph, and Giulietta Capuleti, Ghibelline. Via Arche Scaligere is believed to be the site of Romeo's house and although this may or may not be true, it does house one of Verona's most interesting restaurants, *Arche*, specialising in fish from nearby Chioggia.

The Gioco family have run a restaurant on this site since 1897 and the actual building dates from 1420. Originally, it was a posting inn providing travellers with food, lodging and a change of horse. Today, it is an elegant restaurant serving superb food prepared by Giancarlo Gioci, great-grandson of the founder. The austere dining room is divided into intimate areas by low cane screens and the tables are set with tulip glasses and silver.

The antipasto list is very tempting and I have enjoyed here prawns wrapped in flaky pastry served in a fresh pea sauce and an unusual mussel salad served with local black truffles *alla Vivaldi*. The first course offers a choice of soups, risotto and pasta, but I can't resist *tagliolini alle seppie nere con gamberi di fiume* – a beautifully arranged plate of fresh black pasta served with crayfish. After the first course a lemon sorbet is served with an unusual sage sauce. For the main course there is a very good selection of fish and shellfish, and I warmly recommend the tepid salad of lobster and *rucola* (rocket or arugula), and the sea bass or bream cooked with *funghi porcini*. The dessert trolley offers a rich array, the Austrian influence obvious in the presence of *sachertorte* and *strudel*. The meal ends with fresh fruit and tiny pastries which are accompanied by a delicious glass of Pineau des Charentes.

Arche has a very fine wine list which includes great wines from Italy and France as well as a thorough regional selection. One suggestion to try is the local Lugana Fratelli Zenato from nearby Pechiera at Lake Garda.

Price: Expensive; Amex
Closed: Sunday, Monday lunch; part of July
Location: Central Verona

Osteria La Fontanina

Piazzetta Portichetti Fontanelle 3 Verona
Tel: (045) 913305

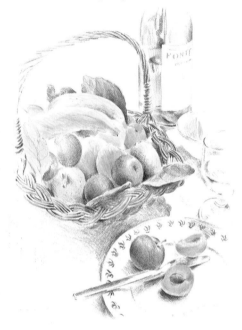

This pretty friendly trattoria seems almost unknown to visitors although it is just 5 minutes from the excellent Due Torri hotel. A few tables are set outside on a flower-decked platform under huge market umbrellas and in cooler weather the inside dining rooms are warmly welcoming. Nicola and Marcello Tapparini serve a daily menu with regional specialities like *bigoli con seppie nere* (pasta with cuttlefish) and home-made pasta with *funghi porcini*. The *gnocchi* are very good, and there are often four or five versions from which to choose. The main course offers a good choice of meat dishes including the local delicacy, horse meat, as well as the more fashionable *carpaccio* (thinly sliced raw beef) and well-prepared veal and beef dishes. There is usually fish prepared in the regional sauce, *saor*, or plainly grilled. A good selection of fairly-priced wines includes a Custoza instead of the better-known Soave, and an Amarone to make a change from Valpolicella and Bardolino.

Price: *Inexpensive; credit cards not accepted*
Closed: *Sunday and 15 days in August*
Location: *S. Stefano area, near church of Sant'Anastasia*

osteria

Non si
effettua
servio
Bar.

Valeggio-sul-Mincio

*B*orghetto in Veleggio-sul-Mincio is a fascinating, romantic backwater with its ruined towers and bridges forming part of the defence line built by the Visconti family in the fourteenth century. When the director, Luchino Visconti, was filming 'Senso', he chose to shoot the battle scenes here.

Antica Locanda Mincio
Borghetto, Valeggio-sul-Mincio
Tel: (045) 7950059

The delightful *Antica Locanda* began life centuries ago as an inn used by local boatmen with oxen-drawn barges, and travellers in post-chaises wanting refreshments and a change of horses.

In 1919 Angelo Bertaiola, grandfather of the present owner, Gabriele, turned his back on agriculture to turn the *Antica Locanda* into a trattoria. He soon attracted customers from nearby Verona and Mantua for Sunday outings to enjoy good home-cooking in an unusually beautiful setting. In warm weather tables are set out on the river bank under the shade of the ancient horse-chestnut and lime trees, and in colder months fires are lit in huge fireplaces in the pleasant dining rooms, with their cheerful frescoes.

The menu contains all the good local specialities like fresh *tortelli*, stuffed with pumpkin, and tagliatelle served with *funghi porcini*. Local free-range chickens are grilled over an open wood fire, and trout and eels from Lake Garda are cooked in many ways. I remember ordering a grilled salmon steak with some misgivings, but I was served a moist, perfectly-cooked piece of salmon, which went very well with an interesting radicchio salad.

There is good house wine, a fair wine list and an extremely good selection of *grappa*.

Price: *Inexpensive; credit cards not accepted*
Closed: *Wednesday evening, Thursday*
Location: *25 km from Verona, 25 km from Mantua*

Mantua

*M*antua, where Romeo languished in banishment, has fortunately escaped mass tourism despite the many interesting sights to be visited in this charming, lakeside town. The Gonzaga family were enlightened rulers for many centuries and under their patronage the culinary arts flourished. Today Mantua proudly upholds this gastronomic heritage.

Aquila Nigra
Vicolo Bonacolsi 4, Mantua
Tel: (0376) 350651

This restaurant is housed in the old stable block of the Palazzo Bonacolsi, just off the main Piazza Sordello. The rectangular dining room has a beamed ceiling, austere pale ochre walls and painted arches. I admired the beautifully-presented antipasti and started my last meal with two perfect pinwheels made from finely seasoned and rolled fillets of eel from the local lake. This was followed by a small portion of pasta, *bigoli*, served with a rich amber sauce made from borlotti beans flavoured with rosemary. For the main course there is a wide choice of fish and meat, but this is a good place to try the delicious cutlets of sturgeon from the Po fish farms. There is a good wine list and the local Colli Morenici wines are very pleasant.

Price: Moderate; Amex
Closed: Sunday evening, Monday; Christmas, part of August
Location: central Mantua, near Piazza Sordello

Il Cigno
Piazza dell'Arco, Mantua
Tel: (0376) 327101

This elegant restaurant is set in a beautiful old building with a cool, perfumed garden. Gaetano Martini offers a set menu and an *a la carte* selection which changes daily. Here you can try eel served with fragrant aromatic vinegar or delicious *culatello* (the most choice part of a *prosciutto*). For the first course there are light innovations like melon soup or the time-honoured *tortelli di zucca*, pasta stuffed with pumpkin. The main course offers the sumptuous Gonzagan recipe for salad of capon breasts. There is an excellent wine list.

Price: Moderate to expensive; Amex, Diners
Closed: Monday, Tuesday evening; part of January and August
Location: central Mantua

MILAN
to Bologna

*M*ilan may be La Scala, the Duomo and the Via Montenapoleone yet music, religion and fashion are only a part of this complex city's life. The heritage of Lombardy moneylenders has made Milan an important banking centre and the many trade fairs keep hotel rooms at a constant premium. The prosperity of Milan has attracted workers from the poorer, less-industrialised south, and today this frenetic modern city seems to have moved a long way from its origins. The great ruling families, the Visconti and Sforza, helped to make Lombardy a very productive region and Napoleon encouraged his weary soldiers by promising to lead them to 'the smiling vineyards and cornfields of Lombardy'. In the early nineteenth century Stendhal found the Milanese art of enjoying life superior to that of Paris, and he particularly admired Milanese cooking traditionally based on butter, rice, meat and cheese. In Milan cheese is served as a separate course, which is not usually the case in Italy, and this region produces Bel Paese, stracchino, gorgonzola, taleggio and mascarpone.

The Ducal Opera House, before La Scala was built, used to contain a restaurant so that music lovers need not deny themselves the pleasures of the table during a long performance. Berlioz was one of the many foreigners to complain that the clatter of knives and forks drowned most of the arias.

The traditional rich, slow cooking does not fit in with the modern pace of life and some parts of central Milan seem to be sinking under a wave of fast food establishments. At the end of the day, however, the Milanese love of good food prevails and in their non-working hours they make up for former deprivations. The hundred year old gastronomic temple, Peck, has inspired a host of other food shops and in the area around Via Spadari, Via Victor Hugo, Via Speronari and Via Cantu, nearly every other shop sells fresh gourmet specialities. Milan boasts innumerable good

restaurants and every region of Italy is represented. Increasingly it is more difficult to find the typical cooking of Lombardy which still appears in the smaller towns nearby.

At Cassinetta di Lugagnano, twenty kilometres from Milan, Ezio Santin has his excellent *Antica Osteria del Ponte*. His style of cooking is highly individual with no clear regional characteristics but this luxury restaurant has won wide acclaim. (Tel. 02 9420034) Closed Sunday and Monday. A meal here could be combined with a visit to the almost unknown small town of Vigevano with its beautiful fifteenth century Piazza Ducale.

Most of the towns in central Italy have some affinity with the cooking of Emilia-Romagna, to the south of Lombardy. The great nineteenth century culinary expert, Artusi, said, "When you hear Bolognese cooking mentioned drop a curtsy, for it deserves it." Bologna has had a tremendous influence on regional cooking and Parma has exerted a similar sway. The cooking of Emilia is rich and smooth, based on butter, Parmesan cheese and fresh egg pasta. Romagna contributes a more robust element, making good use of the Adriatic fish, rabbit, goose and chicken. The meeting point for all this geographical area is really the humble pig which here becomes sublime. There is a Parmesan proverb: *I maiale è come la musica di Verdi: non c'è nulla da buttare via*. (The pig is like Verdi's music, there is nothing that can be thrown away.) Here you can enjoy incomparable Parma ham which is often hand-massaged to improve its texture; *culatello* – the lean pear-shaped cut from the rump which has to be carefully cured by local craftsmen since it is impossible to mass produce; the large boiling sausages like *cotechino* and *zampone* and the innumerable types of salame. Bologna has been manufacturing *mortadella* since the fourteenth century and in some parts of the world it is known simply as 'bologna'. There is a rather indigestible *salame da sugo* which was believed to be an aphrodisiac. Even today it is obligatory at local wedding celebrations and is inevitably the cause of some heartburn. The sizeable Jewish population has produced pork substitutes like goose *proscuitto*, as well as turkey meatballs.

This is the area which has given us *aceto balsamico* (aged aromatic vinegar). This was first produced around Modena using the Trebbiano grape. The process is extremely long and expensive but the final nectar adds a masterly touch to many 'new' creative dishes. Commercially produced bottles give little idea of the flavour of the real thing.

In Milan, Bologna and most of Northern Italy, mealtimes are relatively early, with lunch usually from 12.30 and dinner at 8-8.30 p.m.

San Marino
Via Regina Nuova 64, 22010 Laglio (Como)
Tel. (031) 40 30 83

Around Lake Como and the other Italian lakes, it is not always easy to find a restaurant where the food and service match the splendid view. During the last few years two young brothers, Luigi and Moreno Ruggeri, have won a reputation for offering all three at San Marino in the village of Laglio, ten minutes drive north of Como on the west shore of the lake. In summer you sit out on a terrace above the lake; all winter the scene unfolds beyond picture windows.

The two brothers' aim is to provide fresh, light food, with special emphasis on fresh vegetables and fish, at very reasonable prices. Although there is a printed menu, it is best to ask Luigi, who looks after the guests, what brother Moreno, in the kitchen, is proposing that day. To begin with, it may be vegetable soufflé with a bottom layer of spinach, a layer of fontina cheese in the middle and tomato on top, with a basil sauce. Then pasta with asparagus, zucchini or, more usually, a nettle (*ortiche*) sauce.

For the main course (*secondo piatti*) you may find both fresh lake and sea fish: halibut (*rombo*) salmon (*salmone*) or sturgeon (*storione*). Moreno Ruggeri offers sturgeon with a sauce of mustard, cream and chives,or *branzino* (sea bass) with a white wine, cream and nettle sauce as his favourite specialities.

The wine list is unpretentious and good value, with most wines costing under 20,000 lire.

Price: Inexpensive; Amex
Closed: Only Christmas Day evening
Location: just north of Como on right to Menaggio

Savini

Galleria Vittorio Emanuele II, 20121 Milan
Tel. (02) 8058343

Savini is almost as old as the republic of Italy. The restaurant in Milan's great arcade, the Galleria Vittorio Emanuele II, opened in 1867 and has become one of the institutions of the city. On first nights at La Scala opera, singers and many of their audience repair here for dinner after the performance to find the restaurant filled with flowers, staying open very late to welcome them.

Indeed, this is a restaurant in the grand style with excellent friendly service. The food is tailored to the season and what is in the market. The menu actually changes twice daily; one for lunch, one for dinner, depending on what is available. Thus, in September, the time for great (cep) mushrooms, we were greeted by *pappardelle alla crema con funghi porchini freschi*, among the pasta, or *insalata di funghi porcini* (mushroom salad) or *filetti di vitello con funghi porchini freschi* (veal with fresh ceps).

All the pasta is hand-made on the premises. Being in Milan the risotto is a natural speciality; try *risotto al radicchio di Treviso* (rice with radicchio). And do not hesitate to ask for a favourite pasta sauce or risotto blend, because the menu is largely a basis for discussion and, every pasta or risotto is made to order.

The fish can be wonderful. If you are looking for something light as a main dish take the sea bass (*branzino*) lightly grilled (broiled) and served simply with oil and lemon. But, as befits such a restaurant, there is always a good choice of veal, lamb and beef, such as *carpaccio alla Savini* (thinly sliced raw beef).

For a more serious meal, however, take your time, not just on ordering the food, but to study the list of nearly 400 wines, a rare cross-section of the best of Italian vineyards. Among the sparkling wine is Ferrare Riserva Guilio Ferrari, and among the reds Barolo Collina Rionda, Serralunge d'Alba. There is also an ample selection of cheaper wines such as Dolcetto d'Alba.

Price: Expensive; Amex, Diners, Visa
Closed: Sunday; middle two weeks of August through Christmas/New Year
Location: central Milan

207

Arturo
Via San Marco 22/24, Milan
Tel. (02) 6597653

An unpretentious eating-place near the centre of Milan where it is possible to eat very well for a very modest sum counts as a find. In 1965 Arturo and Maria Maggi took over a *latteria* (a bar licensed to re-sell milk) but today a number of tables have been packed around the counter to provide seating for about thirty people. You sit wherever you find a space with no standing on ceremony, and in a busy city like Milan, where there is little human contact, this is an added bonus. Marco and Roberto help their parents and the warm family atmosphere provides a fitting setting for Arturo's good cooking, which places great importance on light, healthy food with little reference to the cream he sells in the *latteria*.

Fresh vegetables are used with great skill and each day he presents a different vegetable soup using ingredients like fennel, nettles, Jerusalem artichokes or the more common cauliflower or carrots. I remember a particularly delicious zucchini soup. He offers two or three pasta dishes each day as well as a popular *riso freddo*. A good selection of cheeses appears on the menu and Arturo makes very good use of the best buys of fish and meat. His polpettine are legendary and the plain grilled meat shows the exciting vegetable dishes off to advantage. Maria makes some good homemade desserts and the house wine is very pleasant.

Arturo loves roses and his walls are covered with paintings chosen for their subject rather than their artistic merit. He makes an infusion called 'Arturosa' from rose petals which he claims will cure headaches and aid the circulation. This can be sampled at the end of the meal.

Do not seek out *Arturo* if you want an intimate, romantic meal, but do come if you want to enjoy good cooking in an unusual simple setting.

Meals are served from 12.00 to 2.30 pm and from 7.30 to 9.30 pm.

Price: *Inexpensive; no credit cards*
Closed: *Saturday, Sunday*
Location: *central Milan*

Aimo e Nadia
Via Montecuccoli 6, Milan
Tel. (02) 416886

Aimo e Nadia in the suburbs of Milan is one of my favourite restaurants. The setting is calm, the service attentive and food imaginative, beautifully prepared and very easily digested. However, what contributes to the success of this restaurant for me is the personality of Aimo and Nadia Moroni.

Aimo was forced by general post-war poverty to leave his family and native Tuscany when he was only 12 years old to try to earn a living in Milan. He sold chestnuts in winter and ice cream in summer for two years until he got a chance to work as a dishwasher, and he earned extra money carrying the shopping at the market for a Neapolitan hotel chef. From this chef Aimo learned to select good vegetables, fish and meat and he regards this as the most important thing he ever learned. He opened a modest trattoria in 1955 with the help of his mother, who had always been a good cook making the most of very meagre ingredients. When Aimo married Nadia in the early sixties his success was assured. They have together developed complementary skills and built up a serene, harmonious working relationship. Nadia talks about her cooking and reveals the care and love she brings to her work. Aimo creates dishes that are subtle and new, but based on an innate feeling for tradition.

In the middle of the day a set business lunch is served which offers a wide choice for every course. On a recent visit I enjoyed some toasted brioche with *funghi porcini* pâté while waiting for my starter. I was torn between my favourite marrow flowers stuffed with shrimps and ricotta cheese and the *melanzane* (aubergine or egg-plant) fillets rolled and stuffed with mozzarella. Aimo very understandingly spoiled me with one of each and I went on to eat a most delicious spaghetti served with tomatoes, chilli, spring onions and herbs. The sauce was very subtle but with so much genuine goodness I found myself eating with a beatific smile on my face. I followed this with an excellent fillet of *cernia* flavoured with thyme and black olives. Throughout the meal I drank a delicious Chardonnay La Selve and finished with a sorbet made from the fragrant strawberry-flavoured grapes *uva fragola*.

Price: Moderate; Amex
Closed: Saturday lunch and Sunday; August
Location: in the Lorenteggio area, 15 minute taxi from centre

L'Ulmet
Via Disciplini/Via Olmetto, Milan
Tel. (02) 8059260

Situated in 'old' Milan, near the basilico of San Lorenzo, this is one of the most attractive restaurants in the city. The building was once a Sforza coach-house and in the dining-room with its fifteenth century beamed ceiling and fine old furniture, the beautifully set tables are carefully spaced out around an old fireplace. Enrico Mooney is an intriguing mixture of Italian, Red Indian and Irish and his professional expertise comes from a family hotel tradition and a long training in Switzerland, Germany and London.

In 1985, '*L'Ulmet*' opened as a family venture and Enrico's wife and daughter help in the dining-room. His two very young sons, Alessandro and Giovanni, are responsible for the unusual bread, light fresh pasta and delicious pastries. There is a fixed price for each course with usually six to eight dishes offered in each section. The antipasti selection can include various home-produced types of ham and salame, a sweet-sour capon and pomegranate salad or prawns wrapped in flaky pastry served with a vegetable and saffron sauce. The first course usually offers one or two soups like the delicate *crema di zucca* (pumpkin) or *minestra d'orzo, patate e porri*, made from barley, potatoes and leeks. As you would imagine in Milan, there is always an excellent risotto and some delicious pasta. I have enjoyed *taglierini* with scallops and grained mustard sauce and vegetable-stuffed ravioli served in a sweet pepper sauce. The main course offers meat, game and fresh and sea water fish, including fillets of *persico* (perch) served simply with sage and butter, an unusual salmon and broccoli combination and tender *pré-salé* lamb in a subtle thyme sauce. Dessert lovers are presented with an agonising choice and they will deliberate long over the raspberry soufflé, the pancakes with honey and pine nuts and the lavender and aniseed icecream.

Ask Enrico to help you choose the perfect wine to complement your meal. When his wine cellar was excavated a beautiful Roman vaulted ceiling was revealed which now spans an outstanding collection of about 8000 wines from over 200 different areas, including France and California.

Price: Moderate; Amex
Closed: Sunday, Monday lunch; August
Location: central Milan, near San Lorenzo

Cremona

Cremona is famous as the birthplace of Stradivarius and the International School of Violin Making.

Ristorante Ceresole
Via Ceresole 9, Cremona
Tel. (0372) 23322

A few steps from the main square with its eighteenth century *duomo* and bell tower, the Torrazzo, Rino and Saverio Botte, two brothers from Basilicato in the south of Italy, have opened an elegant restaurant. Their wives, Lucia and Anna, do the cooking and the food is an interesting mixture of north and south, old and new. The local influence is seen in the splendid *culatello* and *cotechino* served with *mostarda di pera*, a Cremonese speciality preserve made from whole fruit in a sweet and sour mustard syrup. Among the delicious choices for first course, is a good soup made from *funghi porcini* and barley and a delicate ravioli stuffed with sea bass. The *pietanza bianca* is a sixteenth century local dish. Among the unusual desserts are *spuma di terrone in salsa di nocciole* made with the famous local nougat and pear mousse served in a hot chocolate sauce. There is an interesting wine list.

Price: *Moderate to expensive; Amex, Diners, Visa*
Closed: *Sunday evening and Monday; three weeks in August*
Location: *near main square, Cremona*

~ RECIPE ~
Sogliola con Basilico e Pinoli
Sole with basil and pine nuts from Ceresole

4 sole, each weighing approx 300 g/10 oz, filleted
30 g/10 oz (½ cup) pine nuts
10 g/½ oz (¼ cup) fresh basil
salt, black pepper, juice of ½ lemon
150 ml/¼ pint/⅔ cup olive oil
400 g/ 14 oz potatoes

Roll up the fillets of sole and marinate in the oil, lemon, basil, pine nuts, salt and pepper. Leave for one hour. Cook the fillets in the marinade in an oven (150 degrees C) for 15 minutes. Boil the potatoes. Check the fillets and if necessary moisten with a little white wine during the cooking. Serves 4.

Piacenza

*P*iacenza was founded by the Romans at the end of the important highway, the Via Emilia, and its later history was linked to the fortunes of the ruling Farnese family. Today it is a prosperous small town and many of the old houses contain peaceful gardens which can be glimpsed through the fine courtyards.

Antica Osteria del Teatro

Via Verde 16, Piacenza
Tel. (0523) 23777

This elegant restaurant, housed in a beautifully-restored fifteenth century building is visually striking with its exposed bricks, beamed ceilings, modern spot lights and tall throne-like chairs. Franco Ilari worked for over twenty years with private families and exclusive clubs before opening his restaurant and his professional expertise is revealed in the smooth service and superb presentation. He enjoys gilding the lily and his fresh pasta is used in a myriad of unusual ways. At Easter, using a wooden stencil he makes individual pasta chickens complete with rosemary twig legs. The light filling is topped with an egg and in the time taken to cook the pasta – three minutes – the white becomes firm while the yolk remains liquid to spill out with the first delicious fork full.

The *Antica Osteria* has a regional menu offering stuffed pasta *tortelli dei Farnese* and other local specialities, and an elaborate *menu degustazione* (gastronomic menu) which enables Franco's partner, the young Piacenza-born Filippo Chiappini Dattilo, who studied engineering for three years before succumbing to his passion for cooking, to reveal the virtuosity he developed in France, working under many of the great names.

There is a good selection of desserts and if figs are in season you should not miss the delicious fig mousse. Great French and Italian wines appear in the excellent wine list and Franco is always happy to suggest some less well-known but interesting discovery.

Price: *Moderate to expensive; Amex, Visa, Diners*
Closed: *Sunday; part January, August*
Location: *central Piacenza*

Albergo del Sole
Via Trabattani 22, Maleo Tel. (0377) 58142

Franco Colombani's *Sole* at Maleo near Piacenza is not so much a restaurant as a way of life. The fifteenth century inn, next to the crumbling castle, has been in the family since 1893 and when his father died the young Franco left his engineering studies to help his mother. Over the years he has become totally involved in *Sole* and he has gradually restored and enlarged the old building. When the last Marchese died without a direct heir, Franco bought many of the castle treasures for his inn. In the kitchen a portrait of one of the castle chefs watches over the massive marble table, also from the castle, on which he prepared so many courtly feasts. A great collection of old and new copper cooking pans, still in regular use, hangs on the wall, and in the main dining-room the long refectory table and huge fireplace with a cooking corner still in use at meal times, give a feeling of comfort and continuity. Franco has a treasured collection of antiquarian cookbooks which he uses regularly, including a hand-written collection of recipes collected over the years by the inn's various cooks. His own beautifully printed *Cucina d'Amore* will one day be a collector's item. All this cultural heritage is reflected in the cooking.

Tradition is respected but Franco likes to experiment and his classical *stracotto* (braised beef) is given a new twist when it is

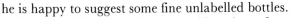

served with vegetables sharpened by an exotic hint of curry. He is famous for his *pasticcio alle ortiche* (pasta with nettle sauce) and his capon salad served with candied lime. Among the many delightful desserts is *sabbiosa* served with mascarpone cream which gets its name from the texture like grains of sand or *sabbia*.

As you would expect from one who used to be the president of the Italian sommeliers, Franco has a great wine cellar and he is happy to suggest some fine unlabelled bottles.

The inn offers several comfortable suites of rooms with old furniture and open fire-places for overnight guests. If you have a chance you should visit Franco's store-room where the precious *aceto balsamico* is aged in a series of wooden barrels, each wood in turn giving a special flavour to the vinegar.

Price: moderate; Amex
Closed: Sunday evening, Monday;
part of January, August
Location: 19 km SE from Piacenza,
60 km from Milan

Parma

Parma is a fascinating city which owes much of its special flavour to Napoleon's second wife, Maria Luigia. She founded the lovely pale yellow Teatro Regio and Paganini was her orchestral director. Today the critical Parmigiani's passion for music is equalled only by their passion for politics and food.

Croce di Malta
Borgo Palmia, Parma
Tel. (0521) 35643

In 1984 Arnaldo Zerbibi and Amedea Merlini opened their attractive restaurant in the historic centre of Parma, returning after 22 years in Canada. The old building was once a convent and later an inn where local hotheads plotted sedition, and the assassination of the last Duke of Parma was carried out between courses by one of the 'regulars'. Today the dining rooms are peaceful with dark wood dressers and an interesting collection of *grappa* and herbal liqueurs. The meal starts with delicious *culatello* or a series of hot antipasti like fried little tarts. The handmade pasta is rolled so thinly that the colours of the filling show through, including amber *tortelli* with pumpkin and magenta *cappellotti* with beetroot. Parmesan cooking is very rich and the second course offers substantial dishes like roast veal with an opulent cheese stuffing or chicken fillets cooked with Sauterne and gongonzola cheese.

Price: Moderate; all credit cards
Closed: Sunday; January, February
Location: Central Parma

Ristorante Villa Maria Luigia
Via D. Galaverna 28, Collechio
Tel. (0521) 805489

The Ceci family have turned the old hunting lodge that belonged to Maria Luigia (Napoleon's second wife) into a beautiful restaurant and they are currently transforming the old stable block into comfortable bedrooms for overnight guests. The menu changes daily but usually includes some specialities like the *soffiata di zucca*, pumpkin soufflé served with a basil sauce and the *scrigno*, little jewel caskets of pasta, in which little pots of tagliatelle

216

with a green vegetable sauce are covered by puff pastry.

Sampling a little Parmesan cheese is almost obligatory and the custom is to eat it with your fingers.

Price: Moderate to expensive; Amex, Diners, Visa
Closed: Thursdays, part of August
Location: 10 km S from Parma

Bologna

Bologna, an Italian city almost bypassed by tourists, is known as *'La Dotta'* (the learned) for its university which is the oldest in Europe, and *'La Grassa'* (the fat) for its rich culinary tradition which is famous throughout the world. However, the ubiquitous *spaghetti bolognese* is a travesty of Bologna cooking. In the authentic dish light yellow tagliatelle are served with an opulent sauce which has little in common with its insipid international namesake.

Silverio
Via Nosadella 37A, Bologna
Tel. (051) 330604

Silverio Cineri has sited his restaurant in Via Nosadella where in the past those in need were given a charitable hot meal and a night's lodging. This seems very appropriate because the hospitable Silverio loves to feed people. However he is very much a working chef and only emerges from his kitchen at the end of the evening. Franco Poli ensures that the service is perfect and he is happy to give expert advice when it comes to selecting wines from Silverio's superb wine list.

Silverio is an imaginative chef who creates new dishes and adds a subtle twist to traditional favourites. I have fond memories of an unusual pasta dish with bitter *cicoria* called poetically *amari ricordi* (bitter memories).

Silverio has a great collection of *aceto balsamico* (aged aromatic vinegar) and some bottles are over one hundred years old. A few drops of this nectar transforms a simple fillet steak into something very special and cheese enthusiasts should be sure to try the parmesan cheese with the 1855 balsamico.

Price: Moderate; all major credit cards
Closed: Monday; August
Location: Central Bologna

Tre Frecce
Strada Maggiore 19, Bologna
Tel. (051) 231200

This restaurant is housed in a thirteenth century building with high, beamed ceilings, huge, old oil paintings and wrought iron lights. In this medieval setting Enzio and Annalisa Salsini serve a delightful mixture of new and traditional food. The menu changes each month and there is something to please everyone. The antipasti course may offer a typical plate of *prosciutto*, *salame* and *mortadella*, a warm salad of shrimps and spinach, *bresaola* (cured beef) with *rughetta* (rocket or arugula) and vinaigrette, or a light terrine made with peas, beans and zucchini, served in a fresh tomato and basil sauce. The pasta course may offer *tagliatelle alla bolognese*, *garganelli romagnoli* (fresh pasta formed with a sort of comb) with zucchini and mint or fillets of *melanzane* (aubergines or egg-plants) stuffed with fine tagliolini. There is a good choice of fish and meat dishes and a delectable array of desserts.

Among the very good wines is a white Pignoletto Colline Bolognese which is very refreshing, and among the reds a full-bodied Sangiovese. The fizzy red Lambrusco is believed to be a great aid to the digestion alongside rich Bolognese cooking.

Price: *Moderate to expensive; Amex, Visa, Diners*
Closed: *Sunday evening, and Monday*
Location: *Central Bologna*

Da Angelo
Via Enrico Mattei 22, Bologna
Tel. (051) 530128

This restaurant is not in the centre but pasta lovers will feel the short taxi ride justified when they see the pasta selection that is on offer. After a few preliminary tasty nibbles, small plates of pasta are brought to the table one after another and you can try as many as you can manage, from a selection which includes tagliatelle with mushrooms, pasta stuffed with chicken breast and asparagus, wide ribbons of white and green pasta with a sweet pepper sauce and pasta stuffed with ricotta and *rughetta* (rocket or arugula). The main course offers an interesting dish of chicken breast in pastry or small pieces of veal served with asparagus in a *sangiovese* wine sauce. A good selection of desserts includes apple tart or *panna cotta* (a custard) with raspberries, or fresh fruit in season

Price: Inexpensive, Amex, Diners
Closed: Sunday; Christmas
Location: 15 minutes by taxi from centre

Cesari
Via de' Carbonesi 9, Bologna
Tel. (051) 237710

The Cesari family who run this welcoming restaurant are also local wine producers. The atmosphere is relaxed and friendly, the service is smilingly efficient and the menu caters for all tastes, with traditional tagliatelle for the conservative, and lighter pasta with asparagus or wild radicchio for those wanting innovations. Paolino Cesari likes to add a new variation to some traditional dishes and he changes menu according to the best produce in the local market. A good place to go to enjoy the feeling of 'old Bologna', where you find tables of regulars enjoying the good food and wide range of family wines.

Price: Moderate; Amex, Diners
Closed: Sunday; Saturdays in July and August
Location: Central Bologna

Brisighella

A few kilometres from Faenza and Ravenna, with their splendid ceramics and mosaics, is the small town of Brisighella, with a restaurant worth a special stop.

La Grotta
Via Metelli 1, Brisighella
Tel. (0546) 81829

Nerio Raccagni, who comes from a strong family tradition of restaurateurs has created an unusual, attractive osteria in a real grotto in Brisighella. Nerio has been involved nearly all his life with food and wine and he has acquired a vast store of cultural and gastronomic expertise. This makes him a fascinating host and he and his young chef, Antonio Casedio, present the best of the region's produce. I have enjoyed ravioli stuffed with scallops and leeks, tagliolini with asparagus and prawns and a delicate guinea fowl studded with truffles. The desserts are equally good and I remember a Bavarian cream made with chestnuts and hazelnuts. If you are lucky you will be offered some of the local cheese which is matured underground (a legacy of the frequent Saracen raids which caused the local people to hide their food) until Saint

Catherine's day towards the end of November. Nerio has a great collection of wine and you would do well to put yourself in his hands in choosing a bottle to complement your meal.

Price: Inexpensive to moderate; credit cards not accepted
Closed: Tuesday; part of January and June
Location: 12 km SW of Faenza

Imola

*I*mola, home of the Ferrari motor works and international motor race, also houses one of Italy's most prestigious restaurants.

San Domenico
Via Sacchi 1, Imola
Tel. (0542) 29000

San Domenico was opened in 1970 by Gianluigi Morini in the same medieval house, near the abbey cloisters, where he himself had been born. Originally his own interests drew him to Rome and a career in the film world but after his marriage his wife Renza suggested opening a restaurant, and eventually Gianluigi Morini managed to persuade the great chef, Nino Bergese, to leave his retirement to pass on his art to one chosen pupil. Nino Bergese had cooked for the House of Savoy, and written the cook-book, *Mangiare da Re* (Royal Recipes). The idea of moulding a young chef and gaining a sort of immortality proved tempting, and he did just that. Today, his last pupil, Valentino Marcattili, keeps Nino Bergese alive with every dish he prepares for the daily menu.

From the large selection of antipasti I have enjoyed here a masterly, simple combination of potatoes, scallops and chives and a delicate dish of smoked goose served with zucchini and walnut oil. Among the first courses I remember a large single *raviolo*, topped with an egg and shavings of white truffle, and this was followed by halibut in a sweet pepper sauce. I finished with a delicious Harlequin Bavarian cream. The wine list reads like a fairy tale and it is simple to find any accompaniment to the meal which is always a magical feast.

Price: Expensive; Amex, Diners, Visa
Closed: Monday; part of January, part of August
Location: 33 km SE from Bologna

Index

INDEX

ROMA

NAPOLI

ISCHIA

CAPRI